PAMELA WESTLAND

Bean Feast

PANTHER
Granada Publishing

Panther Books
Granada Publishing Ltd
8 Grafton Street, London W1X 3LA

Published by Panther Books 1981
Reprinted 1982, 1984

A Granada Paperback Original

Copyright © Pamela Westland 1981

ISBN 0-583-13167-0

Printed and bound in Great Britain by
Collins, Glasgow

Set in Monotype Imprint

Ten years ago Pamela Westland left London and her job as editor of a women's monthly magazine to live in the country with her husband, Douglas, and five cats and 'just write books'. Her first cookery book, *A Taste of the Country*, was a wistful look at what she had been missing – the joy of cooking with all the home-grown fruit, vegetables and herbs a small town garden couldn't provide. Gradually what began as nostalgia has grown into a campaign, and all her cookery books have a message – to use the best possible natural ingredients, cooked in the most convenient way. 'Save time by using modern appliances by all means,' she says, 'but don't squander your family's health by using processed-out foods.'

Her two most recent books illustrate this point perfectly. in *The Complete Grill Cookbook* she shows how contact grills and sandwich makers can produce 'real food' that anyone would be proud of – and indeed, Pamela used only those appliances during the time she was writing the book – and that included Christmas! And in the *The High-Fibre Vegetarian Cookbook* she pioneers for the health awareness that her grandmother, a professional cook, quite naturally took for granted.

B.
Dutch Pea Soup. 46.

By the same author

Contents

Introduction

Throughout history, beans have played a vital part in man's survival, valued as a rich source of protein and other nutrients. They dry and store well and so, ever since prehistorical times, have been recognized as the perfect food to bridge the gap between one harvest and the next. In this form, they are deeply woven into the national cuisine of every culture in the world.

They had other uses, too. Dried bean seeds were the voting instruments in political elections in Greece and Rome and, more widely, were used as both currency and game counters. Their significance is still recalled in our colloquial speech today. Someone who 'knows how many beans make five' is considered knowledgeable and astute. And the poor man who 'hasn't got a bean' is penniless.

Beans are reassuringly easy to grow, produce a display of decorative flowers and an abundant pick-and-come again crop. From the tallest varieties of runner beans to the dwarf forms of French beans, there are plants to suit gardens of all sizes, and even balconies and window boxes, for they can be grown in troughs and tubs, too. And whilst you cannot actually produce flourishing beanstalks on the kitchen windowsill, even there you can raise a worthwhile crop of fresh bean sprouts indoors.

You can follow time-honoured methods and lay in stocks of your own crops, preserving them by drying, bottling, pickling, salting and freezing; but not before you have enjoyed them to the full, young and fresh from the plants. Or you can buy your beans ready cooked – in Britain we are among the world's largest consumers of canned baked beans.

Fresh or preserved, beans offer a culinary versatility unmatched, surely, by any other plant. The recipes which follow give a glimpse of their possibilities, in soups, salads, starters, as main-dish accompaniments, in vegetable dishes of enormous variety, and combined with meat and fish in casseroles and roasts.

As the world faces the dilemma of an increasing protein shortage, beans will continue to be one of the most important crops we grow and still, in some continents, truly the means of survival. And as more of us choose to exclude animal proteins from our diet, we turn to beans for both nourishment and variety. As I hope the recipes in this book show, beans will not fail us.

It is important to bear in mind that most dried beans and peas are interchangeable. A dish that features red kidney beans will be no less tasty or interesting if, for example, haricot beans are substituted. And a dish calling for fresh French beans will be none the less appealing, usually, if frozen ones are used instead. And when time is a prime consideration, as it so often is, canned beans can perfectly well be used where dried ones are indicated; with all the soaking and cooking done for you, the saving in time is often worth the extra cost.

1 What Beans Means Around the World

What beans used to mean to all the civilizations of the ancient world, and still do to under-developed countries today, can be summed up in a single word – survival. In Europe, the Near East and Middle East it was the broad bean; in the New World of the Americas and the West Indies the kidney or French bean; in the Far East the soya and green mung bean. Whatever their size, shape or colour, and in whatever language, beans have been valued from earliest times as part of every nation's survival kit.

Beans means survival because beans also, quite simply, means protein, which is necessary to rebuild body tissue – about 1–2 per cent is replaced in the human body each day. Proteins are composed of hundreds of amino acids, some of which, because they cannot be manufactured in the body, are described as 'essential' acids. (Others are termed 'non-essential'.) Essential amino acids cannot be stored in the body – they are converted into fat or given off as energy – and so they must be eaten in the same meal. Dried beans and peas, that is pulses, are rich in protein (weight for weight, they have a higher protein content than meat) although only soya beans join meat, fish, eggs and dairy products as first-class protein foods, containing all the amino acids the body needs. In addition, pulses are also a rich source of iron and mineral salts. It is easy to understand the part they played in the diet of peoples who could not obtain or afford meat, or whose religion forbade it.

And as if by instinct most cultures around the world have developed their own dishes that represent a perfect food balance, for when pulses are combined with cereals, seeds or dairy produce to supply the amino acid that beans or peas lack, then there is a perfect partnership. Even the humble British breakfast or snack food, beans on toast, gets the formula right: beans plus cereal in the (preferably wholemeal) bread. The traditional American dish of lima beans and corn, *succotash* (see page 152) with or without meat; *kitchri* (see page 105), the Indian forerunner of kedgeree, originally a lightly-spiced blend of mung beans and brown rice, and the many Italian and Greek pulse-plus-pasta dishes, of which *pastitio* (see page 132) is a delicious example, are all complete protein meals.

The nineteenth-century chronicler, Alexander Neckham, illustrates the dependence on pods and seeds of the British countryman. Describing the peasants' 'mess of potage', the pot of broth, vegetables and herbs that, for centuries so to speak, hung all day long over an open fire, he lists the ingredients as 'lentils, peas, beans with pods, beans without pods and frizzled beans' – those that had been dried over the fire in a heated spoon. In another drying process, called somewhat onomatopoeically 'canebyns', the bean pods were soaked for a couple of days, dried out in a tin box over a fire, hulled, chopped into chunks, fried over the fire and dried again. After this laborious drying process – made necessary by the elusive quality of the sun as a drying agent – the beans were considered proof against sprouting and fermentation if the over-wintering storage conditions were a trifle damp.

Dried beans were virtually the only protein food allowable in Europe throughout the Middle Ages on the Wednesdays, Fridays, Saturdays and Lenten fastdays when not even fish was permitted. They would be cooked in a bubbling cauldron; mashed to a purée; ground into a paste known as bean butter, a poor man's substitute for the almond butter which, in wealthier circles, was made into sweetmeats with milk, honey and wine; or ground into meal and mixed with rye, wheat or barley flour for bread. In those years of precarious and precious cereal harvests, the proportion of pulse flour in bread rose in inverse proportion to the income group. It was found that if boiling water were used to mix the bread dough it would go some way towards combating the sourness of the pea flour; but the foul-tasting bean flour was beyond such gentle artifice.

According to Herodotus, the fifth century BC Greek historian and writer, Egyptian priests had regarded beans in any form as unclean, and Pythagoras brought them further into disrepute by claiming that they caused insomnia and unpleasant dreams. But – swings and roundabouts – the Romans were so conscious of their nutritive properties that they offered them in thanksgiving to their gods.

Intermittently throughout history, beans have been used as a currency. Not just bartered for another commodity by the sackful – though they were – but shelled out by the handful, like putting money on the table. Because they are easy to store, transport and count out singly, they have a lot going for them as a monetary system; they just lack the rarity value of gold and silver. The memory of their function lingers on. 'I haven't got a bean,' is to be hard up, indeed. Just as some beans found their way into the cash boxes of earlier civilizations, others were dropped into the ballot boxes, for in Greek and Roman times they were used, instead of crosses on bits of paper, in elections. A white bean signified a 'yes' vote and a black one meant 'no'. And so when Pythagoras told a man to abstain from beans, he was not making a dietary prohibition, but was telling him to stay out of politics.

Ancient pearl merchants in the Middle East, seeking a standard weight by which to measure gemstones, discovered that the dried seeds of the Carob tree, the locust beans, were of an exceptionally uniform weight. Thus the seeds, known as carats, became the universal unit of weight. Diamonds and other precious stones are still referred to by their weight in carats, although more accurate means of measuring have long since been used.

Beans from the New World

The kidney bean in all its various forms and colours – red, yellow, purple, white, green, pink, brown, black, speckled and spotted – was the native bean of Central and South America, and quite unknown in Europe until the New World was explored in the sixteenth century. Indeed, it was one of the culinary treasures that rewarded adventurers who had gone there in search of other riches.

In France they took up the kidney bean with such enthusiasm that it became popularly known as the French bean, while they in turn called it by their generic word for bean, *haricot*, and put it into their *ragoûts*, or *haricots*, of mutton. One particular variety, with long, slender, pale-green seeds, so sweet and tender, is held to be the king of all beans. This the French called *flageolet*, because the pods resemble a flute. We can usually only buy them canned or dried.

The French bean was brought to England by Huguenot refugees in Elizabeth I's reign, and gratefully acknowledged to be more versatile than the native broad bean. The Italians took to them, too, and developed a novel way of cooking them, with garlic and olive oil, in a Chianti bottle immersed in a pot of simmering water – a local adaptation of the energy-saving one-pot cooking. During the nineteenth century, these beans were held to have other health-giving properties besides those of nutrition. The powder made from dried beans was taken as an aid to strengthening kidneys, and the beans were eaten to relieve shortness of breath.

Whilst Europeans incorporated kidney beans into their local dishes in ways that allowed the full flavour and texture of the seeds to be appreciated, countries of the New World continued to serve them in fiery sauces pungent with indigenous spices. Whether they were called *habichuelas* in Puerto Rico, *frijoles* in Mexico, or *caraotas* in Venezuela, the traveller could be sure of a palate-searing experience as he warily dipped a pancake, the traditional *tortilla*, into a sauce swimming with beans and burning hot with chillies.

Owing nothing to modern nutritional sciences, age-old recipes of the American continent abound with their own examples of perfect dietary partnerships. The Cuban dish, *Moros y Christianos* (Moors and Christians) (see page 92) is a lively contrast of *frijoles negros* (black beans) and rice, with tomatoes, onion, garlic and green pepper, and *congris* is a similar concoction made with red kidney beans. In the Barbadian dish, *jug-jug* (see page 155), said to be a corruption of haggis introduced to the island by exiled Scots in the seventeenth century, the pulse is fresh green pigeon peas, known locally as gungo peas, and the seed is ground millet.

Beans from Asia

No such protein compensations are needed in the Asian countries where the soya bean has been the lifeline for centuries. The soya bean is the richest of all in vegetable protein, contains acids that compare exactly with those the human body needs, has a relatively high fat content and is low in starch – which make it economically the most significant bean in the world. Forecasts of a dangerous shortage of world protein in the future must in time make it more significant still.

The soya bean crops up in a variety of high-protein guises, many of them well known to European vegetarians. Soya flour, finely ground and pale lemon in colour, can be used instead of cereal flour as a thickening agent and substituted in bread dough and cake mixtures. Take care to use it only in small quantities, however, for it is not too well endowed with raising properties and tends to give a rather flat and heavy result. Miso, a thick paste made from fermented beans, is added to stews and soups, and imparts a flavour similar to a stock cube. Soya sauce and its Japanese equivalent, *tamari*, made from whole soya beans and salt, are flavouring agents which, for most of us in the West, characterize an Oriental meal.

The taste for bean curd is perhaps less internationally acquired as yet, though even the Chinese do not pretend that the thick little cubes of this custard-like substance are eaten for their grace and flavour. They are simply another means of introducing protein, this time in a form that will take up the taste of meat, vegetables or spices in a sauce. Dried bean curd skin, looking like honey-coloured vanilla bean pods, is sold in thin, stiff strips and needs soaking in water or another liquid before being added to more appealing ingredients.

The Western world is well advanced in its own experiments in harnessing the protein content of soya beans, and has developed a meat substitute called textured vegetable protein, TVP. Under various brand names, in minced or chunk form, the product is seen at present as a 'meat extender', to add to, say, spaghetti sauce or steak and kidney pie in a meat diet, as a meat substitute in vegetarian diets or, in Jewish cuisine, in meals that contain a dairy food. A dish of minced or chunky

TVP and red kidney beans, a sort of *chilli sans carne*, would be one of the most protein-packed dishes one could think of.

The soya bean has one more culinary triumph up its sleeve. It can be stored in its dried state practically indefinitely, and then has only to be introduced to a little water for a few days to burst forth, all crisp and crunchy, into sparkling white and delicious fresh bean sprouts. We can easily grow these for ourselves in a jar in the kitchen (see growing details in the Appendix), or buy them fresh or canned in health food shops and larger supermarkets. Bean sprouts are a familiar ingredient in the crispy little rolled pancakes, the 'spring rolls' served in many Chinese restaurants in the West.

The green mung bean, the native bean of India, which is also cultivated in China, blazes forth into bean sprouts in just the same way. Indeed, being considerably smaller, mung beans have an even shorter growing time. The mung bean has served the peoples of the Indian continent as their daily bread from time immemorial. The ground meal is used for chappatis, pancakes, batters and sweet dishes. Cooked and mashed into a purée, and lightly or generously spiced, the beans have been scooped up at every mealtime, sometimes as a vegetable part of meat or fish dishes, often as the main ingredient in a vegetarian masterpiece.

Split peas, yellow peas, red lentils and peas, call them what you will – *dhal*, *channa*, *masur* and *matar* – have become familiar to us through Indian restaurants, but few Westerners would consider making a meal of a vegetable purée alone. However, nothing but good would apparently come of it. We are told by Ovington, a seventeenth-century traveller, that the high protein content of the Hindu meatless diet resulted in their having 'comely and proportionate bodies' and 'quick and nimble minds'. As if that weren't enough, their comprehension of things was 'easier' (than that of Englishmen?), they had developed a fearlessness of spirit, and had great expectations of longevity – if hunger did not tragically intervene.

When is a bean not a bean?

The distinction between beans and peas is sometimes rather obscured. Iron Age finds at Glastonbury of what are now identified as Celtic beans were thought at first to be peas, they were so small and round. In Jamaica, kidney beans are confusingly called gungo peas. The French-speaking islands of the West Indies do not help: they refer to all beans generically as *pois*.

For centuries peas, like beans, were always eaten in their dried form. Old English cookery books list them by the handful, tied in linen and suspended in the cauldron to swell and absorb the flavours of the pot. But these nutritious legumes were not the preserve of peasants alone. King Edward VII heartily enjoyed a slice of pease pudding as an accompaniment to a plate of pickled or boiled pork.

It was not until the sixteenth century that fresh garden peas found their way from Italy across Northern Europe, and it was another hundred years before they became fashionable in England. Ladies of the French Court were already wild about them, as a letter written in the closing years of the seventeenth century by Madame de Maintenon shows. 'Having supped with the King, and supped well', she says, the ladies would retire to their rooms not to rest but to feast themselves gleefully on dishes of *petits pois*. 'It is all the rage'.

Then there are the peas which, like French and runner beans, are eaten complete with the pod. The sugar pea, or mange-tout pea, which is eaten very young and tender and before the seeds develop, was highly praised by the botanist, Gerard, in his derivative *Herbal* as 'an exceeding delicate meate' which was distinguished from other peas because it could be eaten 'cods and all the rest'. Asparagus peas, too, can be eaten in their entirety, and provided that they are picked soon enough, they have a subtle, almost elusive taste of the vegetable from which they take their name.

It is a far cry from these innocent, juvenile peas to the small, round corn-coloured chick peas which figure extensively in the cuisines of the North African countries, right through the Mediterranean and as far away as India. In Spain and Mexico, these *garbanzos* are laced with spiced *chorizo* sausage, red and green peppers and tomatoes; in Greece and Turkey *hummus* (see page 74), a cross between a dip and a pâté, is made from the pea purée mixed with olive oil and sesame seed paste and, still in Greece, casseroles of these *revythia* are so delicately flavoured with mountain herbs, olive oil and local wine that who needs meat? In Tunisia the hard little chick pea balls provide a clever contrast of texture as a garnish to the soft and downy couscous, and in both Israel and Egypt, in rissoles called falafel (see page 112), chick pea purée is mixed with parsley and onion, lightly spiced with coriander, and shaped into patties.

What all this adds up to is that wherever you go in the world, beans means survival. It also means highly imaginative and exciting cooking, too.

Before luxuriating in the countless ways of using beans and peas in dishes ranging from soups to salads, casseroles to curries, it is as well to brush up on the simple and straight-forward ways of cooking both fresh and preserved beans.

There are four basic ways of cooking fresh beans and peas: boiling, simmering, steaming and Chinese stir-frying. The latter three methods in particular all have the advantage of cooking the vegetables to tender perfection, without loss of valuable nutrients, texture or colour. And then there are the many developments of these methods, when beans or peas are cooked with other vegetables, or given sauces, dressings and toppings that make each dish a feast. Those recipes are in the following chapters.

Preparing the vegetables

RUNNER BEANS

Unlike most of our European neighbours, we in Britain seem to prefer the larger, often coarser, runner bean to the French or green bean. And, sadly, we often leave the beans far too long on the plants, until they are tough and stringy. This gives them an unfair reputation, because runner beans *can* be succulent and tender, if they are picked soon enough. But tell that to a greengrocer!

All but the youngest and tenderest of runner beans need slicing – quite a task if you have a heavy crop. Since you have to use a small, sharp knife to top and tail the beans and usually also to remove the strings from the sides, some people find it quick and easy to continue slicing with the knife, as part of the same operation. Youngish ones can be sliced diagonally, into diamond shapes. To cut the beans into thin slices I find a dual-purpose little hand gadget very helpful, a swivel-action potato peeler which has four thin cutting blades set into a small frame in the handle. For a larger production line, and always when preparing beans for freezing, I use a bean slicer, which clamps to the kitchen table and copes with two beans simultaneously. The slicing attachments to electric mixers and food preparation systems are geared to coping with bountiful home crops or bargain market buys, too. So the choice is yours. If you have the time, and find it relaxing, slice away with a knife. If every moment is precious and you have the equipment, marvel in modern technology and watch a river of bean slices flowing as fast as you can feed the machine.

Young runner beans, or older ones which have been cut into chunks or sliced, can be cooked in the same ways as French beans: by boiling, steaming or stir-frying.

FRENCH BEANS

Young French beans simply need topping and tailing. Some varieties are stringless, but for those that are not, older and larger beans need stringing in the same way as runner beans. If they are large, break them in half (which gives rise to the alternative name of snap beans) or cut them straight across into chunks about 5 cm (2 in) long.

Cook French beans by boiling, steaming or stir-frying.

BROAD BEANS

One of the most delicious ways to serve broad beans is whole, in the pod. To do this, the pods must be very young and tender, no more than 10–12 cm (4–5 in) long. Top and tail the pods and cut them diagonally across into three or four pieces. Cook them as soon as possible after picking and leave them to soak meanwhile in a bowl of cold water, so that they stay crisp.

Larger than that, the beans should be podded, and the pods discarded. Very large broad bean seeds have tough outer skins which should be popped off when they are cooked. Broad beans quickly lose colour, so prepare them just before cooking and put them in a bowl of water acidulated with vinegar or lemon juice.

Whole broad beans may be cooked by boiling, simmering, steaming or stir-frying, the seeds by boiling, simmering or stir-frying.

BEAN SPROUTS

There is no need to wash bean sprouts you have grown yourself, nor to remove the seed husks. To keep them fresh, store them *in water* in a covered bowl in the refrigerator, changing the water each day. To refresh canned bean sprouts drain them into a colander and rinse them thoroughly in cold, running water, then leave them in water.

Raw sprouts are excellent in salads. Otherwise, they need very little cooking. They can, however, be boiled, simmered or cooked in their own special Chinese way, by stir-frying.

FRESH SOYA BEANS

As soya beans are not a native crop in Britain, fresh bean pods are not readily available in the shops. You can treat the young pods as French beans, top and tail them and cook them by boiling, steaming or stir-frying.

The pods are difficult to open once they are past the very young stage. Blanch the whole pods in boiling water for 5 minutes, drain them, then 'pop' them.

PEAS

Fresh home-grown peas are one of the delights of the table, and must not be allowed to become just a childhood memory.

Shell the peas and put them in a bowl of cold water. Pick them over and discard any maggoty ones and those that float to the top. Reserve the pods (unless they are old and withered) for *green pea pod soup* (see page 40).

Peas may be cooked by boiling (not the best method), simmering, steaming – especially in the classic French way, with the heart of a lettuce – or stir-frying.

MANGE-TOUT PEAS

As the name tells us, these are the ones you eat whole, pods and seeds together. Though to be strictly accurate, they are best eaten when the seeds have scarcely developed, and the pods are flat. Top and tail the pods. Very young ones can be served raw in salad, with a French dressing. More mature pods might need stringing in the same way as beans. When you cut off the top, continue tearing off the string along one side in the same action.

Mange-tout peas may be boiled, simmered, steamed or – perhaps most delicious of all – stir-fried.

ASPARAGUS PEAS

These are a disaster if they are not harvested when they are very small. Pick them when the pods are no more than 3–5 cm (1–2 in) long, then top and tail them. After that they are almost irretrievably tough.

Cook the pods by simmering, steaming or stir-frying.

DRIED BEANS AND PEAS

Pulses are found by some people to be indigestible, or to give rise to unsocial noises – recognized in Arab countries as expressions of culinary appreciation. Dried beans and peas give off many of these disturbing gases in the rehydration process, during the initial soaking period. They also give off soluble vitamins during this period, too. By discarding the soaking water, you get rid of some of the 'anti-social' gases, but sacrifice the vitamins. Since as a nation we are not deficient in vitamin-rich foods, this might be a sacrifice worth making.

Beans and peas that you have dried at home from your own crop and are using in a relatively short time will need less soaking and cooking than ones that have been in store for months or even years. For although pulses do store remarkably well, as time goes on they lose more moisture and take longer to prepare. When you buy pulses, of course, you cannot know this, and so it is best to be on the safe side, give them a good long soaking and allow the longer of the suggested cooking times.

First, wash the pulses in a bowl of cold water. Pick them over and remove any pieces of grit. Discard any beans or peas that float to the top or appear badly discoloured.

The traditional and 'slow' method of soaking most pulses is to put them in a bowl with cold water and leave them for several hours – all day or overnight. As the pulses absorb about two-and-a-half times their volume in moisture, allow 3 cups of water to 1 cup of beans and a roomy container. You can speed up the process by putting the pulses in hot or warm water, and for the toughest ones, soya beans and chick peas, add a good pinch of bicarbonate of soda. Butter beans, green peas and split peas need less time, only 2–3 hours; lentils do not need soaking, but should be washed.

A much quicker method is to put the pulses in a pan with hot water, bring it to the boil, cover the pan and boil for 2 minutes. Remove the pan from the heat and leave the pulses to cool in the water. Drain them, and they are ready to cook.

Cooking fresh vegetables

BOILING

In a sense, boiling is the most difficult of the cooking methods, because it can cause most disappointments, if the vegetables are overcooked and lose texture, flavour or colour – or all three.

Have a very little salted water fast-boiling in a pan over a high heat – just enough to cover the vegetables. Drop the prepared vegetables in and bring the water, still over high heat, quickly back to the boil. Reduce the heat to medium and continue cooking with the lid tilted. The vegetables should never be cooked until they are soft. The secret is to serve them when they are just slightly resistant to the bite – 'al dente', as the Italians describe it. Drain the beans into a colander and run cold water through them to stop any further cooking. The times given below are a general guide, but can vary according to the age and quality of the crop.

Whole young runner beans, whole French beans	12–15 minutes
Sliced broad bean pods	10–12 minutes
Broad bean seeds	8–12 minutes
Sliced runner beans, cut French beans	5–8 minutes
Peas (add sugar and mint to flavour)	10–12 minutes
Mange-tout peas	2 minutes

Bean sprouts should be plunged into boiling salted water, brought back to the boil, then drained.

Beans and peas that have been boiled will have a rather lacklustre look. Restore the gloss by reheating them gently in melted butter, a tablespoon or so of double or single cream, or natural yoghurt. Beans can have the added interest of a little fresh chopped or dried parsley or marjoram stirred in just before serving, and peas a little fresh chopped or dried mint. A tablespoon of chopped shallot or spring onion stirred in with the butter glaze, and a final sprinkling of ground black pepper are good with both beans and peas.

Other garnishes for beans include chopped walnuts, halved almonds fried in butter and cubes of crisply-fried bacon, or breadcrumbs fried in butter until they are dry.

SIMMERING

A delicious way to cook some vegetables is to simmer them in a very little chicken stock and butter over a low heat, until they have absorbed the liquor and the flavour, and are just tender and shiny. Broad beans, bean sprouts, peas, mange-tout peas and asparagus peas can all be cooked in this way; runner beans and French beans are less suitable.

For four servings, allow about 90 ml (6 tablespoons) of chicken stock, or water and a piece of stock cube, and 50 g (2 oz) butter. Put them in a small pan with a little salt if necessary (taste the stock to check) and a few grindings of black pepper. Add the vegetables and bring the liquor just to the boil, then cover the pan and keep it at simmering point until the vegetables are just tender – from 12–15 minutes, according to size, age and type. To give more flavour to peas, you can add a sprig of fresh mint or 2·5 ml ($\frac{1}{2}$ teaspoon) dried mint and a little sugar. Glaze the cooked vegetables with a small knob of extra butter and season with salt, pepper and chopped herbs.

STEAMING

This age-old method of cooking is enjoying a well-deserved revival. Country cooks have always been in favour of steaming vegetables, because it does not 'take the goodness out of them'. It takes a little longer than boiling, but pays dividends in terms of flavour.

A steaming pan, in which the top pan, with a perforated base, fits snugly over the lower one, is ideal but not necessary. You can use a steaming fan, a perforated metal disc with folding perforated flaps which open out to fit inside any round pan over 15 cm (6 in) in diameter; you can fit a colander into a large pan, or simply put a small heatproof shallow bowl or dish on a trivet in a pan of boiling water.

Since the vegetables cook by steam and not by direct contact with the heat or water, the water in the base pan must be boiling rapidly before the beans or peas are added, and kept at a steady rolling boil throughout.

Put the prepared beans or peas on a heated dish with a knob of butter and a good sprinkling of salt and pepper. Stir to coat them well, then put the dish in the steamer or pan. Cover with a well-fitting lid (or press a piece of foil over the top) and keep the water boiling for 15-20 minutes, according to the type of vegetable. Or you can put the vegetables with the butter and seasonings on a piece of foil, double-seal the edges all round and put the parcel in the steamer or on a trivet in a pan of boiling water. Allow about 5 minutes longer, for the heat to penetrate the foil.

If you are using the oven for the rest of the meal, you might prefer to utilize the heat to cook the vegetables. Wrap peas or beans in foil with butter and seasonings, and bake them at medium heat. Peas take 20 minutes, broad beans 25 minutes, and sliced runner beans or whole French beans 30 minutes. Frozen beans and peas in foil take 25-35 minutes either in the oven or steamed.

Garnish steamed vegetables with butter, seasoning and herbs, or with the toppings suggested for those cooked by boiling.

STIR-FRYING

Anyone who has ever enjoyed a dish of stir-fried fresh vegetables in a good Chinese restaurant will know how delicious they are. Quickly fried in very hot oil or fat for a very short time, then simmered in their own moisture or a little added stock or seasoning, the vegetables retain nutrition, flavour and colour. It's a perfect way to cook beans and peas of all types, as well as interesting combinations of vegetables.

The traditional Chinese utensil for stir-frying is a *wok*, a conical-shaped pan that fits over the top of a gas ring. However, a heavy-based frying-pan is a good substitute, and

Western cooks should not be discouraged for want of a pan with sloping sides.

For the purpose of stir-frying, vegetables are divided into three categories, soft, semi-hard and hard. Soft vegetables are those with the highest moisture content that require the shortest cooking time. Bean sprouts are an example. Semi-hard and hard vegetables take a little longer to cook, and need a little added moisture, usually water or chicken stock. Mange-tout peas, shelled peas and young broad bean seeds are semi-hard vegetables. Hard vegetables, which take more cooking, include runner beans, French beans and young broad beans cooked in the pod.

One of the arts of Chinese cooking, and stir-frying is no exception, is in the preparation of the food. Time saved in cooking is often spent one stage earlier – in cutting or chopping all but the smallest vegetables into exactly even-sized pieces. Top, tail and string runner beans, then chop them into small diagonal pieces no more than 2.5 cm (1 in) long. Top and tail French beans, string them if necessary, and cut them into small straight pieces about 4 cm (1½ in) long; you can leave very small ones whole. Top and tail very small broad bean pods and cut them on a slant about 4 cm (1½ in) long. Use only the youngest mange-tout peas for cooking by this method. Top and tail them, remove any strings, and cook them whole. Top and tail asparagus peas and leave them whole. Shell peas and larger broad beans as usual. Wash all vegetables and drain them in a colander.

Use a good quality vegetable oil, such as peanut oil, or lard, but not olive oil, which has too much flavour. Heat the dry pan over a medium heat, turn the heat up high and add 45 ml (3 tablespoons) of oil or 25 g (1 oz) lard for four servings. Heat the oil until it is very hot but not smoking, then add 2.5 ml (½ teaspoon) of salt (this preserves the green colour of vegetables), and a flavouring such as a thinly-sliced garlic clove, a 5-cm (2-in) piece finely chopped fresh root ginger, 4 finely chopped spring onions or 2 chopped shallots. Now add the vegetables a few at a time, so that the temperature of the oil is maintained, and stir them for 1 minute, then lower the heat to medium again.

Bean sprouts, which are soft vegetables, will need stir-frying for no more than another 2 minutes, and will then be ready to serve. However, they are improved by added seasoning. Mix 30 ml (2 tablespoons) soya sauce, dry sherry, sake or vinegar with 5 ml (1 teaspoon) sugar, and pour it into the pan. Stir, still over medium heat, until it is just heated through. Transfer the bean sprouts to a heated serving dish and serve them very hot.

To cook semi-hard and hard vegetables, add 150 ml ($\frac{1}{4}$ pint) chicken stock or water after the initial 1 minute of stir-frying. Stir well and cover the pan. Cook mange-tout peas, shelled peas and broad beans for a further 3 minutes, and runner beans, French beans and broad beans in the pod for up to 5 minutes, without lifting the lid. Now add the seasoning as described and stir until it is hot and completely blended with the vegetables. Cook without the lid to evaporate any excess moisture, then transfer the vegetables to a heated serving dish.

To cut down on-the-spot cooking time, you can blanch the vegetables before stir-frying, or cook thawed frozen vegetables in this way – which gives them a tremendous lift from the run-of-the-mill presentation. Drained, canned vegetables can be stir-fried, too, with the initial flavouring of garlic, shallot or spring onion. As soon as they are coated with the oil, go straight on to the final stage and add the seasoning.

Cooking dried beans and peas

BOILING

It is difficult to be precise about cooking times for pulses, since some seed varieties take longer than others; some will be 'fresher' than others, and so on. But luckily, as all pulses are particularly good-tempered and do not collapse with gentle over-cooking, it is best to err on the side of allowing too much time.

Put the soaked pulses into a pan with enough water, vegetable stock or chicken stock to cover. Never add salt at this stage, it inhibits cooking and toughens them. Add the salt just before the end of cooking time, or at the very end, then leave the pan to mellow on the top of the stove for a few minutes.

Flavour the cooking liquor, if you like, with a bay leaf, celery, parsley stalks or other fresh herbs, an onion or a couple of shallots stuck with a few cloves, or a clove of garlic, and season it with black pepper. In hard-water areas, you can add a good pinch of bicarbonate of soda when cooking toughies such as soya beans or chick peas. When cooking dried green peas, substitute mint for the other herbs, and add a little sugar to the water. Bring the liquor to the boil and simmer for the following times. Or cook the pulses in your pressure cooker, or a crock-pot, following the directions for your own appliance.

1 hour or 10 minutes at high pressure
   Lentils
   Mung beans
   Split peas

1–1½ hours or 15 minutes at high pressure
   Aduki beans
   Butter beans or lima beans
   Flageolets
   Haricot (white) beans
   Kidney or navy beans

1–2½ hours or 20 minutes at high pressure
   Black-eyed beans
   Borlotti beans
   Broad beans or fava beans
   Pinto beans

2–3 hours or 35 minutes at high pressure
   Black beans or turtle beans
   Gungo peas
   Whole peas

3–3½ hours or 45 minutes at high pressure
   Chick peas
   Soya beans

CROCK-POT
The long, slow cooking achieved in an electric crock-pot is ideal for all soaked pulses. It is advisable, however, partly to

cook the firmest ones before cooking them in the pot. Bring
them to the boil in a saucepan, simmer them in the convention-
al way for $\frac{1}{2}$–1 hour, then put them in the crock-pot. Follow the
times given in the booklet for your appliance – the wattage
varies from one model to another.

SLOW OVEN

Crock-pots are the modern equivalent of slow oven cooking,
when a dish would be left in the oven all day or overnight, to
simmer gently to perfection. If you have a solid-fuel or oil-fired
cooker that is always burning, you will find it economical to
cook pulses in a casserole at the lowest heat for several hours.
Heat the stock first, add the beans, herbs and other flavourings,
cover the casserole and simmer for about 8 hours.

3 Preserving for the Future

Anyone who is really into beans, and particularly those of us who grow our own, will not be satisfied with enjoying them only in the summer, at harvest time, delicious though they are then. We will want to do what our ancestors always did, and preserve them in all kinds of ways, so that we can have a bean feast at any time of the year.

Luckily, this could not be easier. It is for this very reason that beans and peas were so highly prized in historical times – because they had such a wonderfully promising future, and could be preserved by a variety of methods for use through the barren winter months.

Even before modern methods of preservation were known, housewives were kept busy laying in stores of this protein-rich food. The seeds were dried in the sun until all the moisture was drawn off and there was no longer any risk of mould developing; the pods were strung up and dried, most decoratively, in the sun until they rattled like paper chains; French and runner beans were sliced and layered in jars with salt to keep for months on the pantry shelves – literally 'salted away' for the winter; beans and peas, some podded, some sliced, were bottled or pickled in preserving jars, and beans could be added to other vegetables in chutneys.

Canning was introduced as the 'new' way to preserve food at the beginning of the nineteenth century, and this method now enables us to enjoy produce ranging from delicately sweet *petits pois* and young, tender French beans to every child's favourite, baked beans, the year around. And now we have not only the commercial freezing process, but the means of storing our own garden or market produce at home in sub-zero temperatures.

WHAT WE MEAN BY PRESERVING

All plants are composed of organic matter, and the object in preserving food is to retard or stop the process of decay caused by bacteria, yeasts, moulds, enzymes or oxidation. One way to do this is to reduce the activity of water in the plant material. We can do this by drying, salting or freezing, or by adding vinegar, as in pickling. Another way is to sterilize the food, by heating, as we do in bottling.

DRYING

People long ago discovered that once the water in vegetables had evaporated, the growth of enzymes was arrested. Looking along the packed rows of shelves in health food shops or supermarkets, we can be glad of this, for the drying process gives us our store-cupboard of aduki beans, black-eyed peas, red kidney beans, haricot beans and so on. These, of course, are now dried commercially under controlled temperature and humidity conditions, but once upon a time the heat of the sun was enough.

In a good summer, it is satisfying to try the evocative, back-to-nature method and dry seeds or whole beans out in the open over a period of several days. They need a dry heat, and must be brought indoors when the temperature drops at night. If the sun blinks and lets you down, you can carry on the drying in the oven at a very low heat, in the airing cupboard or over an all-night burning stove.

To prepare the vegetables for drying, pod peas and broad beans; de-string and trim French beans and very small runner beans, and slice larger ones. Blanch the vegetables in boiling, salted water for 1–3 minutes according to size, age and type; a little bicarbonate of soda, added in the proportion of 15 g ($\frac{1}{2}$ oz) to 4.5 litres (8 pints) water helps to preserve the green colour. Drain the vegetables in a colander, then toss them gently on a tray covered with crumpled kitchen paper towels.

Or you can do as they still do in Far-Eastern countries, and dry whole or sliced beans in garlands, hanging from tree to tree; in this case thread the beans on twine or thin string, knotting at intervals to allow a good circulation of air, and then blanch the complete garland.

According to the amount of vegetables you are drying, you can use wire-mesh baking cooling trays, garden sieves or slatted trays, covered with clean, soft muslin or cheesecloth. Spread the vegetables out on the trays so that they are not touching each other, cover them with a piece of muslin to protect them from dust and insects, and put them in the full sun for as long each day as possible, turning them over occasionally so that they dry evenly. Bring them in at night, and take them out the next day for their sunbath, until they are rattling dry.

In an ideal world, the sun would always be shining and this method would be practical. Instead, you can put the vegetables to dry in an oven temperature of 50°C (120°F), Gas $\frac{1}{4}$ – gradually increasing the heat to no more than 70°C (150°F) Gas $\frac{1}{2}$ – too much heat will split the skins. You can use a gas cooker with the pilot light ignited or the residual heat of the oven after cooking. Indoor drying can be continuous or intermittent, whichever is more convenient.

Marrowfat peas and haricot beans can be left on the vine or plants to dry. When the pods are crisp pull up the whole plants and leave them under cover in a well-ventilated place, such as a garden shed, for the seeds to ripen. When they are dry, pod the seeds and leave them in open boxes or trays in a dry, airy place for a couple of days.

Leave sun or heat-dried vegetables in the same way for a day or two. Then store them in bottles, jars or polythene boxes with tightly-fitting lids. Strong light affects the quality of dried vegetables, so it is best to keep them in a closed cupboard or to cover glass jars with bands of dark paper.

Before cooking your dried vegetables, soak them overnight in warm water.

SAVING BEANS FOR SEED

It is a satisfying economy to save the seed you have grown yourself to plant for next year's harvest. To do this, set aside some plants especially for the purpose and do not pick any pods at all, but leave them all to ripen. Towards the end of the summer, pull up the whole plants and hang them in a dry, well-ventilated place to finish ripening. Shell out the seeds and store them in boxes where they will not be touched by frost – so the garden shed will probably not be the ideal place.

SALTING

We once bought a house which had a huge pantry with brick floors and marble shelves – and the shelves were stacked with glass jars and earthenware crocks of salted French and runner beans. Eventually, we decided to consume our assets, and though the beans had clearly been stored for longer than the recommended six months, they were still tender and tasty.

Use glass, pottery or earthenware containers, never metal ones. Gather the beans when they are very young, wash them in cold, running water and dry them on crumpled kitchen paper towels. Trim the beans, 'string' runner beans and, if necessary, slice them.

You will need 450 g (1 lb) kitchen salt to each 1.5 kg (3¼ lb) beans. Put a layer of salt in each container, then a layer of beans, and push them well down. Continue layering and firming down, and finish with a layer of salt. Cover the containers and leave for 2 or 3 days, during which time the beans will shrink a little and settle. Add further layers of beans, salt, beans, and finish with salt. Cover the containers with strong polythene, glass lids and spring-clip or screw-band tops – large preserving jars are ideal for salting. Never let metal lids come into contact with the salt. Store the beans in a cool, dry place. To use them, remove just as many as you need with a draining spoon, soak them for 2 hours in warm water, then rinse in cold, running water and drain. Cook in boiling water (no salt) for 20–30 minutes.

BOTTLING

We hear a lot about bottling fruit, much less about bottling vegetables. One reason for this, of course, is that freezing has come to be regarded as *the* way of preserving produce in the home kitchen. It takes less time and trouble than bottling, so has a great deal going for it. Added to that, bottling vegetables needs more care than bottling fruit. Vegetables are low in acid and may contain bacteria which would not be killed by water at boiling temperature. Therefore, a reliable pressure cooker is essential; the ordinary water-bath or oven methods are not suitable. The temperature must be at least 115°C (240°F), so before attempting this process, check the instruction booklet

with your appliance. If you are in doubt about its efficiency, or
your own ability to use it, do not go any further.

Next, check on your store of bottles. They must be preserving jars – jam jars will not withstand the pressure. They must
not be chipped or cracked, and metal lids must not be damaged
or scratched. Be sure that you have an adequate supply of new
rubber rings; once they have been used they stretch and are no
longer completely effective. Wash the jars and lids, rinse them
thoroughly, and you are all set to go.

Since the bottling process is a relatively long one, it is not
worthwhile processing tired, ancient vegetables. Gather tender
young beans and peas, prepare them in the usual way and process them as soon as possible after picking. Pod broad beans
and peas, trim green beans and trim, string and if necessary
slice runner beans. Wash them in cold, running water, then
blanch them in boiling, salted water, 1–2 minutes for peas, 2–3
minutes for French, runner or broad beans, according to age
and size. Drain the vegetables well and pack them tightly but
without crushing into clean, warm jars. Tap the jars as you
fill them to settle the vegetables down and release trapped air.

Dissolve kitchen salt in the proportion of 25 g (1 oz) to each
1 litre (1¾ pints) of water. Bring it to the boil and pour it, still
boiling, into the jars, to within 10 mm (½ in) of the rim. You
can add a little green food colouring to the brine if you wish,
and 25 g (1 oz) of sugar to each 1 litre (1¾ pints) of water for
peas. Put the lids on the jars and fix spring clips. Leave screw-
band tops a half-turn from being fully tightened.

Stand the trivet or a wooden rack in the pressure cooker and
arrange the jars so that they do not touch each other or the
sides – if they do, they might crack. Pour in 5 cm (2 in) of water
and put the cooker on a high heat. Leave the control valve open
for steam to escape for 7–10 minutes, then close the valve and
bring the pressure up to medium (follow the directions for
your own appliance carefully at every stage). Maintain this
pressure for 35 minutes if 450-g (1-lb) bottles are used, and for
5 minutes longer for 1-litre (1¾-pint) jars. Containers larger
than that are not recommended for preserving vegetables in
this way.

When the sterilization process is complete, remove the pres-

sure cooker from the heat and leave it to cool very gradually.
Do not open the control valve until the pressure registers zero,
then remove the lid. Stand the jars on a wooden board or sheets
of newspaper until they are completely cool. When they are
cold, test the lids for a complete seal. If they are sealed, dry
screw bands, rub them inside with oil and screw them on
tightly; remove spring clips. If not, either repeat the sterilization, or use the vegetables straight away. Under no circum-
stances store vegetables that are incorrectly preserved.

To use the vegetables, reheat them in the brine. Any left-over
brine makes a good basic stock for soups, sauces and gravies.

PICKLING

French beans and podded broad beans can be pickled in spiced
vinegar, and make interesting and unusual accompaniments to
cold meats, savoury pies and cheese – ideal for a traditional
farmhouse high tea.

Pick young beans and prepare them in the usual way, topping and tailing French beans, podding broad beans. Blanch
them in boiling, salted water for 3 minutes, then drain them in
a colander.

Meanwhile, prepare the spiced vinegar. You need about 1
litre (1¾ pints) white distilled vinegar or, for a more distinctive
flavour, white wine vinegar, to each 1 kg (2¼ lb) prepared beans.
Put the vinegar into a saucepan with 100 g (4 oz) sugar, 1 large
onion and 3 cloves of garlic, peeled and sliced, 2 bay leaves,
5 ml (1 teaspoon) black peppercorns and 5 ml (1 teaspoon)
mustard seed. Do not use copper or iron saucepans for pickle-
making since they react with vinegar. Bring the vinegar to the
boil, stirring to dissolve the sugar, then simmer it for 30
minutes.

Pack the vegetables into clean, warm preserving jars, stand-
ing French beans upright. Lightly tap the jars to pack the beans
neatly. Strain the vinegar and pour it, still hot, into the jars.
Seal the jars and store them in a cool, dark place.

FREEZING

Some of the other methods of preserving beans and peas are
of almost quaint interest now that so many households have a

freezer, always hungry to store vegetables picked fresh from the garden or bought at peak-season prices in markets or supermarkets. And most people would agree that frozen vegetables come closest in both texture and flavour to fresh ones. So bean harvest-time becomes a scene of frenzied activity as we pick and pod, trim and slice, blanch and drain, pack and label our produce with all the zeal and enthusiasm of squirrels hiding nuts or dogs burying bones in the garden.

Anyone who owns a freezer is sure to have spent many a fascinating hour poring over the instruction booklet, and will probably have read at least one book on the subject, so this is just a brief recap on the technique as it applies to beans and peas.

Again, only the freshest and best of your produce should be frozen. Space is wasted if you freeze vegetables that are 'over the top', and lack of quality will probably be wrongly blamed on the freezing process itself instead of, more accurately, on the selection.

Prepare the vegetables according to type. Pod broad beans and separate them into batches of small, medium and large seeds. Discard any starchy ones. Pod peas, again choosing only the young ones. Do not freeze them if the pods have started to wither and dry on the vine. Wash mange-tout peas, French and runner beans, trim them and remove any strings. Slice large beans. Grade them, too, according to size.

To blanch the vegetables, bring a large pan of salted water to the boil. Add a small quantity of the prepared vegetables and keep the pan over a high heat so that the water quickly returns to the boil. Time the blanching period from this point, following the individual times given in the chart which follows. As soon as the blanching period is up, remove the pan from the heat and quickly transfer the vegetables into ice-cold water so that the blanching process immediately stops. When they are cold, remove the vegetables with a draining spoon and spread them on crumpled kitchen paper to dry. Open-freeze both beans and peas in the fast-freeze section of the freezer on trays or baking dishes. When they are frozen, transfer them to heavy-quality polythene bags or rigid polythene containers, seal the bags, put the lids on the boxes, label and date them. Store in the main compartment of the freezer.

Note: you can freeze French beans and peas without blanching them first, but, as you can see below, they will have a much shorter freezer life.

Vegetable	Blanching Time	Storage Time
Peas	1–2 minutes	Blanched: 12 months
		Unblanched: 3 months
Mange-tout peas	2 minutes	Blanched: 8 months
Broad beans	2–4 minutes	Blanched: 12 months
Sliced runner beans	2 minutes	Blanched: 12 months
Whole French or very young runner beans	3 minutes	Blanched: 12 months
		Unblanched: 2 months

CANNING

It could be said that it was Napoleon who inspired the invention of canning, when he offered a prize of 12,000 francs to anyone who could devise a method of preserving food in an easily transportable form – he had in mind, of course, keeping the French armies well nourished when they were on the march. In 1809 a Frenchman, Nicolas Appert, collected the cash for his method of preserving food in glass containers, and a year later, with no such incentive, an Englishman, Peter Durant, adapted the method to use metal cans. It was not for another fifty years that the method was perfected, and the problems ironed out. Machines were made for domestic use, and larger households took to canning garden produce as a truly cottage industry. But since the machines are no longer made, and are obtainable only from antique shops, it is impractical to suggest canning as a means of preserving our crops.

And anyway, is there any point, when commercial enterprise, with all its skill and know-how, has shown us so clearly what canned beans means?

Baked beans have passed their centenary, for they were probably first canned in 1875, when an American firm in

Portland, Maine, supplied its fishing fleet with cans of 'Boston type' baked beans, flavoured with pork and molasses. In 1880 the recipe for baked beans in tomato sauce was introduced, and these were being canned on a large scale in Indianapolis by 1891. Soon after that, in 1895, the Pittsburgh firm of H. J. Heinz produced its first batch of baked beans with tomato sauce – one of the celebrated 57 varieties of canned goods which that manufacturer marketed.

And now baked beans seem almost part of our way of life. From the State of Michigan alone, the world's largest producer of navy beans for canning and drying, Britain imports 50,000 metric tons a year – and that is only half of our total requirement. When you consider that we eat 700 million cans of baked beans a year, apart from all the other types of canned beans, perhaps it is a little daunting for the home producer to set up in competition!

4 Soups

Beans can be practically all things to all soups. They can add colour, texture and protein to clear vegetable and meat stocks, add thickness and bulk (protein, too, of course) to creamy blended soups, and fill out country broths to a meal in a dish.

In the summer, when they are fresh and tender, bean pods and seeds make light and lovely soups, ideal to introduce a seasonal main course, whether it is hot or cold. Soups have the advantage of making a few vegetables go a long way, so make them if your bean harvest is precious. Try them, too, if you have a bumper crop – fresh bean soups make a complete change from serving beans as a salad or as a main-dish accompaniment.

And in the winter, when dried beans in store provide such a wealth of flavour and goodness, you could produce a different bean soup for each day, such is the enormous variety. A bowl of hot soup has welcomed children home from school and labourers in from the farms in raw weather for centuries past.

Bear in mind that most of the dried beans are completely interchangeable with one another. Check that the cooking times are the same (see pages 21–27) or adjust them accordingly. This way, you will find some exciting new combinations and widen your repertoire.

BEAN SPROUT SOUP

A light, refreshing start to a meal, whether it's Chinese or Western style.

    100 g (4 oz) lean pork
    5 ml (1 teaspoon) rock salt
    15 g (½ oz) cornflour
    1 litre (1¾ pints) chicken stock, or water and stock cube
    225 g (8 oz) fresh bean sprouts (or canned ones, drained and
        rinsed)
    30 ml (2 tablespoons) soya sauce
    15 ml (1 tablespoon) dry sherry
    freshly-ground black pepper

Cut the pork into very thin matchstick strips. Blend the salt and cornflour and toss the pork in the mixture to coat it thoroughly. Pour the chicken stock into a pan and bring it to the boil. Add the pork and simmer briskly for 5 minutes. Add the bean sprouts and bring quickly back to simmering point. Simmer for 2 minutes. Add the soya sauce and sherry, season well with pepper and serve at once.
Serves 4

BROAD BEAN SOUP

A French recipe, in which the basic soup is flavoured with a garlic and herb paste, *pistou*.

    450 g (1 lb) broad beans (shelled weight)
    450 g (1 lb) potatoes, peeled and diced
    450 g (1 lb) tomatoes, skinned
    2 large onions, peeled and sliced
    2.25 litres (4 pints) water
    salt
    100 g (4 oz) pasta shapes
    freshly-ground black pepper

    For the Pistou
    3 large cloves garlic, peeled

10 ml (2 teaspoons) dried basil, or 15 ml (1 tablespoon) fresh
chopped basil, if available
30 ml (2 tablespoons) olive oil
45 ml (3 tablespoons) tomato purée

Put the broad beans, potatoes, tomatoes and onions into a pan
with the water and salt. Bring to the boil, cover the pan and
simmer for 30 minutes. Add the pasta, season with pepper and
continue simmering until the pasta is tender (about 8–12
minutes, depending on the shapes used).

To make the *pistou* paste, pound the garlic cloves with the
basil. Very gradually pour on the oil, working it in thoroughly,
then the tomato purée. Or blend to a paste in a blender.

When the soup is cooked, stir in the *pistou* until it is completely blended, and serve very hot.
Serves 8

GREEN BEAN SOUP

An unusual presentation, from the Basque region of Northern
Spain.

450 g (1 lb) French beans
75 ml (5 tablespoons) olive oil
1 large onion, peeled and sliced
3 cloves garlic, peeled and crushed
1 litre (1¾ pints) water
450 g (1 lb) potatoes, peeled and sliced
salt and freshly-ground black pepper
4 thick slices white bread
75 g (3 oz) cheese, grated

Top and tail the beans and slice them. Heat the oil in a pan
and lightly fry the onion and garlic. Do not let them start to
change colour. Pour in the water, add the beans and potatoes,
and season with salt and pepper. Bring to the boil, cover the
pan and simmer for 45 minutes. The potatoes should pulp and
thicken the soup. Taste and add more seasoning if necessary.

Remove the crusts from the bread, cut the slices into triangles
and sprinkle them with the grated cheese. Pour the soup into a

heated tureen and float the bread on top. If you prefer, you can toast the bread and cheese until the cheese melts, before garnishing the soup.
Serves 4

GREEN PEA POD SOUP

When they're young and green, pea pods make a delightful soup. Do not try this recipe with tired old pods – they have nothing to contribute.

    1 kg (2¼ lb) green peas (total weight)
    50 g (2 oz) butter
    1 large onion, peeled and sliced
    1.25 litres (2¼ pints) water
    1 bay leaf
    a few mint leaves
    300 ml (½ pint) milk
    salt and freshly-ground black pepper
    fresh chopped mint to garnish

Shell the peas and serve the seeds another time. Thoroughly wash the pods. Melt the butter in a large pan and lightly fry the onion until it is just transparent. Put in the pea pods and the water, and add the bay leaf and mint leaves. Bring to the boil, cover the pan and simmer over a low heat until the pods are tender – about 2½ hours. Remove the bay leaf. Liquidize in a blender, then rub the purée through a sieve to remove the strings. Return the purée to the cleaned pan, stir in the milk and season well. Reheat the soup slowly, and serve sprinkled with chopped mint.

On a warm day, you can serve this soup chilled. After adding the milk and seasoning, cool the soup before putting it in a covered container in the refrigerator.

Hot buttered croûtons rolled in chopped mint (see page 45) are a good accompaniment, when serving the soup hot.
Serves 6

GREEN PEA AND LETTUCE SOUP

You can use the dark outer leaves of lettuce for this soup,
reserving the heart to simmer with green peas on another
occasion.

450 g (1 lb) green peas (shelled weight)
25 g (1 oz) butter
12 large lettuce leaves
1 medium-sized onion, peeled and sliced
850 ml (1½ pints) chicken stock
15 ml (1 tablespoon) fresh mint leaves, or 2.5 ml (½ teaspoon)
   dried mint
5 ml (1 teaspoon) sugar
salt and freshly-ground black pepper
fresh chopped mint to garnish (optional)

Put all the ingredients into a pan. Season with salt and pepper
and bring slowly to the boil. Cover the pan and simmer for
25–30 minutes. Liquidize the soup in a blender, or rub through
a sieve. Return the purée to the cleaned pan and adjust seasoning if necessary. Reheat slowly.

Serve with a sprinkling of chopped mint or a small mint
sprig, if available.
Serves 4

GREEN PEA SOUP

If you have a generous crop of peas, you might like to make one
of summer's most delicate soups, which can be served hot or
cold.

50 g (2 oz) butter
1 medium-sized onion, peeled and sliced
3 spring onions, trimmed and sliced
450 g (1 lb) green peas (shelled weight)
— reserve a few pods
a few mint leaves
600 ml (1 pint) chicken stock, or water and stock cube
300 ml (½ pint) milk
salt and freshly-ground black pepper

Melt the butter in a pan and lightly fry the onion and spring onions until they are transparent. Add the peas, a few pods for flavour, and the mint. Pour on the chicken stock and bring to the boil. Cover the pan and simmer for about 15 minutes until the peas are tender. Remove the pods. Liquidize the soup in a blender, or rub through a sieve. Return the purée to the cleaned pan, add the milk and season well. Reheat slowly, stirring occasionally.

Alternatively, cool the soup, put it into a covered container and chill it in the refrigerator.

Garnish with fresh chopped mint or sprigs of mint.

Serves 4

RUNNER BEAN SOUP

A smooth, rich soup, enriched with egg yolk and soured cream.

  450 g (1 lb) runner beans
  1.25 litres (2¼ pints) water
  salt
  1 egg yolk
  30 ml (2 tablespoons) flour
  150 ml (¼ pint) soured cream
  5 ml (1 teaspoon) lemon juice
  salt and freshly-ground black pepper

Top and tail the beans, remove any strings and cut them into chunks. Cook them in the boiling, salted water until tender – about 5–8 minutes. Liquidize the soup in a blender, or rub through a sieve. Return the purée to the cleaned pan and adjust seasoning if necessary.

Beat the egg yolk, flour and most of the soured cream together (reserve a little for garnish) and stir in the lemon juice. Beat this mixture into the bean purée over a low heat. Taste and season with salt and pepper. Stir until it is just at simmering point, but do not boil.

Serve the soup hot, garnished with a trail of soured cream.

Serves 6

SUMMER VEGETABLE SOUP

Quick and easy, the kind of thing to prepare on a day when you don't feel like cooking.

1.25 litres (2¼ pints) chicken stock, or water and stock cubes
salt and freshly-ground black pepper
15 ml (1 tablespoon) soya sauce
225 g (8 oz) fresh bean sprouts (or use canned ones, drained and rinsed)
10-cm (4-in) piece cucumber, very thinly sliced
1 bunch watercress leaves, washed and chopped
30 ml (2 tablespoons) chopped chives
3 tomatoes, skinned and sliced

Heat the chicken stock in a large pan and season it well with salt, pepper and soya sauce. Add all the vegetables, bring the stock to the boil, and simmer for 3–4 minutes. Taste and add more seasoning if necessary.
Serves 4

BEAN GAZPACHO

For a balmy day, an ice-cold soup that's waiting in the refrigerator.

1 kg (2¼ lb) tomatoes, skinned and finely chopped
1 large onion, peeled and thinly sliced
2 green peppers, trimmed and chopped into thin strips
2 cloves garlic, peeled and crushed
100 g (4 oz) fresh white breadcrumbs
1 × 375-g (14-oz) can flageolets or haricot beans, thoroughly drained
60 ml (4 tablespoons) olive oil
45 ml (3 tablespoons) red wine vinegar
150 ml (¼ pint) dry white wine
a few drops of red pepper sauce
825 ml (1½ pints) chicken stock
30 ml (2 tablespoons) fresh chopped parsley
salt and freshly-ground black pepper

Mix all the ingredients together in a large bowl, stir well and season with salt and pepper. Cover the bowl and leave the soup in the refrigerator overnight. Taste and add more seasoning if necessary before serving. The soup should have quite a 'kick' to it.

Serves 6

BLACK BEAN SOUP

Don't expect the soup to be dramatically black – the beans are white under the skin.

225 g (8 oz) dried black beans, soaked
1 ham bone
1.75 litres (3 pints) water
1 large onion, peeled and sliced
2 stalks celery, sliced
1 bay leaf
a few parsley stalks
juice of $\frac{1}{2}$ lemon
salt and freshly-ground black pepper
1 hard-boiled egg, chopped

Drain the beans and put them in a pan with the ham bone and water. Add the prepared vegetables, and the bay leaf and parsley tied together. Bring slowly to the boil, skimming the surface occasionally with a draining spoon. Cover the pan and simmer until the beans are tender – about 3 hours. Remove the ham bone, bay leaf and parsley.

Liquidize the beans and stock in a blender and then strain it, or rub through a sieve. Return the soup to the cleaned pan, stir in the lemon juice and season well. Reheat the soup gently and add a little water or chicken stock if it is too thick.

Serve garnished with the chopped hard-boiled egg.

Serves 5–6

BUTTER BEAN SOUP

Pork and beans in an old-fashioned country way.

175 g (6 oz) salt pork
30 ml (2 tablespoons) vegetable oil

1 large onion, peeled and chopped
2 large cloves garlic, peeled and finely chopped
1.75 litres (3 pints) water
325 g (12 oz) dried butter beans, soaked
1 bay leaf
a few parsley stalks
1 × 375-g (14-oz) can peeled tomatoes
2.5 ml ($\frac{1}{2}$ teaspoon) paprika
salt and freshly-ground black pepper
15 ml (1 tablespoon) fresh chopped parsley

Remove the rind from the pork and cut the meat into small cubes. Heat the oil in a large pan. Fry the pork lightly in the oil until the fat runs, add the onion and garlic, and fry for 2–3 minutes more. Add the water, drained beans, and the bay leaf and parsley tied together. Bring to the boil, cover the pan and simmer for 1 hour. Add the tomatoes and their juice and paprika, taste and adjust the seasoning. Remove the bay leaf and parsley. Gently heat the soup, stirring occasionally. Sprinkle with chopped parsley to garnish.
Serves 6

COUNTRY LENTIL SOUP

Frozen peas added to a traditional red lentil soup give a welcome change of texture.

675 g (1$\frac{1}{2}$ lb) gammon knuckle
175 g (6 oz) dried red lentils, washed
1 large carrot, peeled and sliced
2 stalks celery, chopped
1 medium-sized onion, peeled and sliced
15 ml (1 tablespoon) Worcestershire sauce
1.5 litres (2$\frac{1}{2}$ pints) water
salt and freshly-ground black pepper
100 g (4 oz) frozen peas, thawed

For Croûtons (*optional*)
3 thick slices day-old white bread
40 g (1$\frac{1}{2}$ oz) butter

Soak the knuckle in water overnight. Put the knuckle and

lentils in a large pan with all the remaining ingredients, except the frozen peas. Bring slowly to the boil, skimming the surface occasionally with a draining spoon to remove the scum. Reduce the heat to very low and simmer for 2 hours.

Remove the knuckle from the pan. When the bone is cool enough to handle, remove the meat and cut it into cubes. Liquidize the soup in a blender then strain it, or rub through a sieve. Return the purée to the cleaned pan. Add the cubes of meat and the frozen peas and simmer for 10–15 minutes. Taste and adjust the seasoning, adding salt if necessary.

To make the croûtons, cut the crusts from the bread, and the bread into small cubes. Melt the butter in a frying-pan and fry the bread cubes, turning them once, until they have absorbed all the fat and are golden brown. Sprinkle the croûtons on the soup just before serving, or hand them round separately.
Serves 6–8

DUTCH PEA SOUP

This soup is so filling that it is often served in Holland as a complete meal, with hunks of fresh, crusty bread. It improves in flavour if kept for a day or two.

450 g (1 lb) dried green split peas, washed
450 g (1 lb) gammon knuckle or 2 pigs' trotters
1.75 litres (3 pints) water
2 medium-sized onions, peeled and sliced
3 stalks celery, chopped
30 ml (2 tablespoons) celery leaves, chopped
450 g (1 lb) potatoes, peeled and sliced
15 ml (1 tablespoon) fresh chopped parsley, or 10 ml (2 teaspoons) mixed dried herbs
salt and freshly-ground black pepper
450 ml (¾ pint) milk
75 g (3 oz) butter
1 × 450-g (1 lb) can frankfurters, drained and sliced

Soak the split peas and the knuckles or trotters separately, the peas for at least 2 hours, the knuckle or trotters for 6 hours, or overnight. Drain them both and put them in a large pan with the water. Bring to the boil, skimming the surface occasionally with a draining spoon to remove the scum. Cover and simmer for 1 hour. Add the prepared vegetables and simmer for 1½ hours more.

Remove the knuckle or the trotters with a draining spoon and, when they are cool enough to handle, cut off the meat and return it to the soup. Add the herbs. Taste the soup and then season with salt, if necessary, and pepper. Add the milk and butter and stir over a low heat to blend. Simmer very gently for 30 minutes, then add the sliced frankfurters. Allow them to heat through.

The soup is now ready to serve. It is even better, though, if it is cooled, stored in the refrigerator overnight and gently reheated to serve next day.

Serves 8

FLOATING ISLAND SOUP

Whipped cream floats on top of a wine-rich green pea soup – a lovely dinner-party luxury.

  100 g (4 oz) dried split peas, soaked
  1 small onion, peeled and sliced
  1 stalk celery, chopped
  2 × 300 g (10½-oz) cans condensed consommé
  150 ml (¼ pint) dry sherry
  salt and freshly-ground black pepper
  150 ml (¼ pint) double cream, whipped
  40 g (1½ oz) blanched almonds

Drain the split peas and cook them in boiling water with the onion and celery until tender – about 1 hour. Drain the vegetables and liquidize them in a blender with a little of the consommé, or rub through a sieve. Put the purée in a pan and gradually stir in the consommé over a low heat, adding 1 can of water. Add the sherry and gently heat the soup. Season well with salt and pepper. Serve garnished with swirls of the chilled whipped cream and the toasted almonds.

To toast the almonds, spread them on a piece of foil covering the grill pan. Grill them under a high heat for a few minutes, turning them once.
Serves 4

GARBANZO SOUP

Chick peas, a favourite ingredient in Mediterranean dishes, are combined with spicy sausages in the Spanish way.

    60 ml (4 tablespoons) olive oil
    1 large onion, peeled and sliced
    2 large cloves garlic, peeled and crushed
    1.75 litres (3 pints) water
    450 g (1 lb) chick peas, soaked
    4 large tomatoes, skinned and chopped
    50 g (2 oz) ham, diced
    175 g (6 oz) chorizo sausage, diced
    30 ml (2 tablespoons) fresh chopped parsley
    salt and freshly-ground black pepper

Heat the oil in a large pan and lightly fry the onion and garlic until they are transparent. Add the water and chick peas and bring to the boil. Cover the pan and simmer until the chick peas are tender – about 3 hours. Add the tomatoes, ham, sausage and parsley and season well with salt and pepper. Simmer until the peas are tender.
Serves 6

GREEN LENTIL SOUP

The greeny-brown 'German' lentils give the true rugged texture of this thick country soup.

    675 g (1½ lb) gammon knuckle
    45 ml (3 tablespoons) vegetable oil
    1 large onion, peeled and thinly sliced
    1.5 litres (2½ pints) beef stock, or use water and stock cubes
    175 g (6 oz) green lentils, soaked
    2 bay leaves
    a few parsley stalks

1 large carrot, peeled and thinly sliced
2 stalks celery, chopped
225 g (8 oz) potatoes, peeled and diced
225 g (8 oz) firm, white cabbage, shredded
salt and freshly-ground black pepper

For Cheese Croûtons (optional)
3 thick slices day-old white bread
40 g (1½ oz) butter
25 g (1 oz) Parmesan cheese, grated

Soak the knuckle in water overnight, then strain.

Heat the oil in a large pan and lightly fry the onion over a moderate heat for 4–5 minutes. Pour on the stock, stirring, then add the knuckle, drained lentils, and the bay leaves and parsley tied together. Bring gradually to the boil, skimming the surface occasionally with a draining spoon to remove the scum. Cover the pan and simmer for 45 minutes. Add the prepared vegetables, bring back to the boil and simmer for a further 20 minutes, or until all the vegetables are just tender. Taste the soup and season well with salt and pepper. Remove the bay leaves and parsley. Remove the knuckle from the soup and, when it is cool enough to handle, cut the meat into cubes, and return them to the pan.

Serve hot, sprinkled, if liked, with cheese croûtons.

To make the croûtons, cut the crusts from the bread and cut the bread into cubes. Melt the butter in a frying-pan and fry the cubes, tossing them once, until they are golden brown. Tip the grated cheese on to a piece of greaseproof paper and toss the hot croûtons to cover them.

Serves 6

HARICOT BEAN CHOWDER

An adaptation of an American favourite, clam chowder, using creamy haricot beans.

15 ml (1 tablespoon) vegetable oil
1 large onion, peeled and sliced
4 rashers streaky bacon
100 g (4 oz) dried haricot beans, soaked
1.25 litres (2¼ pints) chicken stock, or water and stock cube
450 g (1 lb) potatoes, peeled and diced
300 ml (½ pint) milk
salt and freshly-ground black pepper
50 g (2 oz) cheddar cheese, grated
15 ml (1 tablespoon) fresh chopped parsley

Heat the oil in a pan and fry the onion over a moderate heat for 3–4 minutes. Remove the rind from the bacon rashers, chop the bacon into pieces and fry it with the onion for another 3 minutes. Add the drained haricot beans and the chicken stock and bring slowly to the boil. Cover the pan, reduce the heat and simmer for 1 hour.

Add the potatoes and the milk to the pan, and season with salt and pepper. Bring the liquor slowly back to the boil, then simmer for a further 15–20 minutes, until both the beans and the potatoes are just tender, but not broken up. Taste for seasoning and add more if necessary.

Serve the chowder topped with grated cheese stirred in at the last moment, and chopped parsley.
Serves 6

JAMAICAN BEAN SOUP

An exotic way to use speckled pink beans, combined with red pepper and a fiery seasoning.

100 g (4 oz) salt pork
450 g (1 lb) dried pinto beans, soaked
1 large onion, peeled and sliced
1 stalk celery, chopped
1 red pepper, trimmed and sliced
5 ml (1 teaspoon) dried thyme

a few celery leaves
a few parsley stalks
2.25 litres (4 pints) water
a few drops red pepper sauce
salt

Cut the rind from the pork, and cut the meat and fat into cubes. Put it into a pan with the drained beans, onion, celery, red pepper and thyme. Tie the celery leaves and parsley stalks together and add them to the pan. Pour on the water, bring to the boil and cover the pan. Simmer until the beans are tender – about 1½–2 hours. Remove the celery and parsley stalks. Liquidize the soup in a blender and strain it if the chopped celery has left 'strings', or rub through a sieve. Return the soup to the cleaned pan, season with pepper sauce and salt to taste, and reheat.
Serves 6

KIDNEY BEAN SOUP

A smooth, meaty soup spiced with hot pepper sauce. With the addition of dumplings it becomes a hearty meal.

450 g (1 lb) dried kidney beans, washed
1 gammon knuckle
3.5 litres (6 pints) water
225 g (8 oz) shin of beef
1 large onion, peeled and chopped
1 large carrot, peeled and sliced
3 spring onions, trimmed and chopped
225 g (8 oz) potatoes, peeled and sliced
5 ml (1 teaspoon) dried thyme
15 ml (3 teaspoons) red pepper sauce
salt

For the Bacon Dumplings (optional)
2 rashers bacon
50 g (2 oz) self-raising flour
pinch of salt
25 g (1 oz) shredded suet
10 ml (2 teaspoons) Worcestershire sauce
cold water to mix

Soak the kidney beans and the knuckle separately, overnight, then drain off the water. Put them in a large pan with the water. Add the shin of beef and bring slowly to the boil, skimming the surface with a draining spoon to remove the scum. Cover the pan and simmer for 1 hour. Add the prepared vegetables, bring back to the boil, and simmer for a further 30 minutes.

Remove the knuckle and beef. When they are cool enough to handle, cut the gammon meat from the bone and cut it and the beef into cubes. Liquidize the soup in a blender, or rub it through a sieve. Return the soup to the cleaned pan, add the cubes of meat, the thyme and pepper sauce. Taste the soup and season with salt if necessary. Bring just to the boil again. If you are making dumplings, add them to the soup at this point, then simmer gently for 15 minutes.

To make the dumplings, cut the rind from the bacon rashers and chop the bacon finely. Fry in a non-stick pan or in a very little fat until crisp. Mix together the flour, salt and suet, stir in the Worcestershire sauce and bacon and gradually pour on just enough cold water to mix to a firm dough. Shape the mixture into balls, dust them with flour and add them to the hot soup. They will sink in the pan at first, but float to the top as they cook.

Serves 8–10

LENTIL AND BACON BROTH

A smooth pulse soup with the hidden flavour of fresh vegetables and orange, a good choice for an informal party.

  25 g (1 oz) butter
  3 rashers smoked bacon
  1 medium-sized onion, peeled and sliced
  1 large carrot, peeled and sliced
  2 stalks celery, chopped
  175 g (6 oz) brown lentils, washed
  1.75 litres (3 pints) chicken stock, or use water and stock
    cubes
  2 bay leaves
  2.5 ml ($\frac{1}{2}$ teaspoon) dried thyme

grated rind of $\frac{1}{2}$ orange
salt and freshly-ground black pepper

Melt the butter in a large pan. Cut the rind from the bacon and chop the bacon into pieces. Fry with the sliced onion for 5 minutes over a medium heat, stirring occasionally. Add the prepared carrots and celery, and stir well. Add the lentils and pour on the chicken stock. Stir again, and bring to the boil. Add the bay leaves, thyme and grated orange rind. Cover the pan, reduce the heat and simmer for $1\frac{1}{2}$ hours. Remove the bay leaves. Taste the soup and season well. Liquidize the soup in a blender then strain it, or rub it through a sieve. Return it to the cleaned pan and reheat gently.
Serves 6

LENTIL AND SPINACH SOUP

Anyone lucky enough to have been offered homely Greek cooking in a private house might have come across this delicious country soup.

225 g (8 oz) green lentils, washed
825 ml ($1\frac{1}{2}$ pints) water
60 ml (4 tablespoons) olive oil, or 40 g ($1\frac{1}{2}$ oz) butter
1 large onion, peeled and sliced
1 large clove garlic, peeled and crushed
2.5 ml ($\frac{1}{2}$ teaspoon) ground cumin
450 g (1 lb) frozen spinach, thawed
salt and freshly-ground black pepper

Put the lentils in a large pan with the water, bring to the boil and cover. Simmer until the lentils are soft – about $\frac{3}{4}$–1 hour.

Meanwhile, heat the oil or butter in a small pan. Fry the onion over a medium heat until it is transparent. Add the garlic, cumin and spinach and mash with a wooden spoon. Season with salt and pepper and heat slowly. Simmer for about 10 minutes. Add the lentils, a little more water if necessary and check the seasoning. If you wish, you can liquidize the soup in a blender, and return the purée to the pan to reheat. But Greek cooks take a pride in the coarse texture and earthy colour combination of the soup as it is.
Serves 4

MIXED VEGETABLE SOUP

Haricot beans contrast well in both shape and texture with fresh seasonal vegetables in a nutritious, colourful soup.

   2 rashers streaky bacon
   1 large onion, peeled and thinly sliced
   1 large carrot, peeled and thinly sliced
   1 small cauliflower, trimmed and cut into florets
   1 × 200-g (7-oz) can peeled tomatoes
   175 g (6 oz) dried haricot beans, soaked
   1.25 litres (2¼ pints) beef stock, or water and stock cubes
   salt and freshly-ground black pepper
   50 g (2 oz) Cheddar cheese, grated

Remove the rind from the bacon and chop the bacon into pieces. Fry them over a low heat in a non-stick pan, stirring until the fat runs. Add the onion and fry gently until it is transparent. Add the carrot and cauliflower, the tomatoes and their juice and the drained beans. Stir well, and pour in the stock, stirring. Bring slowly to the boil, cover the pan, reduce the heat to very low and simmer for 1½ hours. Season with salt and pepper.

Serve the soup hot with grated cheese as a last-minute garnish.
Serves 6

MUNG BEAN AND LEEK SOUP

As green as the countryside in spring, a soup with the refreshing tang of lemon.

   4 rashers streaky bacon
   6 medium-sized leeks, trimmed, well washed and sliced
   1 large clove garlic, peeled and sliced
   1 large carrot, peeled and sliced
   2.25 litres (4 pints) ham or chicken stock, or water and
      chicken stock cubes
   225 g (8 oz) dried mung beans, soaked
   1 lemon
   salt and freshly-ground pepper

Remove the rind from the bacon and chop the bacon into pieces. Fry them over a low heat in a non-stick pan, stirring until the fat runs. Add the prepared vegetables, the stock and the drained beans and bring to the boil. Cover the pan and simmer for about 1 hour. Liquidize the soup in a blender, or rub it through a sieve. Return the purée to the cleaned pan. Add the grated rind and strained juice of the lemon, and season well. Gently reheat the soup.

As a quick and tasty garnish, you might like to try crumbled 'pork scratchings' or bacon-flavoured savoury snacks.
Serves 6

REVYTHIA SOUP

This is the way they make chick pea soup on the Greek Islands.

325 g (12 oz) dried chick peas, soaked
1.5 litres (2½ pints) chicken stock (or just water)
5 ml (1 teaspoon) lemon juice
45 ml (3 tablespoons) olive oil
1 bay leaf
a few parsley stalks
freshly-ground black pepper
2 large onions, peeled and sliced
salt
15 ml (1 tablespoon) fresh chopped parsley

Put the chick peas in a pan with the stock or water and bring to the boil. Add the lemon juice, olive oil, bay leaf and parsley tied together, and the pepper, and return to the boil. Reduce the heat and simmer for 2 hours. Add the onions and salt and simmer for a further 1 hour, or until the peas are tender.

Remove and discard the bay leaf and parsley, then remove about half the chick peas with a draining spoon. Liquidize them in a blender with a little of the stock, or rub them through a sieve. Return this purée to the pan and stir it well to thicken the soup.

Reheat the soup and serve it sprinkled with chopped parsley.
Serves 4

SAUSAGE AND BEAN SOUP

Cheese pastry, quick and easy to make, is an impressive – but optional – accompaniment to this farmhouse soup.

30 ml (2 tablespoons) vegetable oil
2 large onions, peeled and sliced
225 g (8 oz) mushrooms, wiped and sliced
1.25 litres (2¼ pints) beef stock, or use water and stock cubes
a little fat for frying
450 g (1 lb) pork sausages
2 × 275-g (10-oz) cans red kidney beans, drained
salt and freshly-ground black pepper
pinch of cayenne pepper

For Cheese Pastries (optional)
325 g (12 oz) bought puff pastry
1 egg, beaten
50 g (2 oz) Parmesan cheese, grated

Heat the oil in a large pan and fry the onions over a medium heat until they are transparent. Add the mushrooms and fry for 2–3 minutes. Pour on the beef stock and bring slowly to the boil. Simmer for 15 minutes.

Heat a little fat in a frying-pan and lightly fry the sausages. Cut them diagonally into large chunks and add them to the soup with the drained kidney beans. Season well and simmer for 5 minutes. To make a more special course, serve with cheese pastries. Hot, crusty French bread is good, too.

To make the cheese pastries, roll out the puff pastry on a lightly-floured board. Cut into eight squares. Brush with beaten egg and sprinkle with half the cheese. Fold diagonally into triangles. Brush the tops with egg and sprinkle with the remaining cheese. Transfer to a wetted, non-stick baking tray and bake in the oven preheated to 220°C (425°F), Gas 7, for 15–20 minutes, until well risen and golden brown. Serve hot.
Serves 8

SCOTCH BROTH

As evocative as heather on the highlands, a traditional soup
with mutton, dried peas and barley.

100 g (4 oz) dried peas, soaked
675 g (1½ lb) scrag end of mutton (lamb), trimmed of excess
fat
1.75 litres (3 pints) water
50 g (2 oz) pearl barley, washed
2 large leeks, trimmed, well washed and sliced
1 large carrot, peeled and sliced
1 small turnip, peeled and diced
salt and freshly-ground black pepper
15 ml (1 tablespoon) fresh chopped parsley

Put the dried peas in a large pan with the meat, water and barley. Bring to the boil, skimming the surface with a draining
spoon to remove the scum. Cover the pan, reduce the heat and
simmer very gently for 1¼ hours. Add the prepared vegetables,
salt and pepper and bring back to the boil. Simmer for a further
45 minutes. Remove the meat and, when it is cool enough to
handle, cut it into serving-sized pieces and return it to the pan.

Serve the soup very hot, in deep bowls, sprinkled with the
parsley.
Serves 6

VEGETABLE AND PASTA SOUP

Full of interest, colour, nourishment, a soup that's a meal in
itself.

75 g (3 oz) dried red kidney beans, soaked
75 g (3 oz) dried white haricot beans, soaked
1 large onion, peeled and sliced
2.25 litres (4 pints) water
2 large carrots, peeled and sliced
4 stalks celery, sliced
2 cloves garlic, peeled and crushed
225 g (8 oz) potatoes, peeled and diced
1 × 375-g (14-oz) can peeled tomatoes
100 g (4 oz) pasta shells or other shapes
5 ml (1 teaspoon) dried oregano
salt and freshly-ground black pepper
50 g (2 oz) Parmesan cheese, grated

Put the drained beans in a pan with the onion and water. Bring
to the boil, cover the pan and simmer for 1 hour.

Add the carrots, celery, garlic, potatoes, tomatoes and pasta,
and season with the oregano, salt and pepper. Bring slowly to
the boil again, and simmer for 20–25 minutes, until the beans,
potatoes and pasta are just tender. Taste the soup for seasoning,
and adjust if necessary.

Sprinkle the cheese as a last-minute garnish, or serve it
separately. Hot French bread is a good accompaniment.
Serves 6–8

5 Salads and Starters

Beans offer the cook in a hurry some of the most exciting yet simplest ways to start a meal, or accompany the main course. The new season's beans, fresh, young and tender, are as succulent as any salad vegetables and combine with dressings ranging from the cool-as-a-cucumber effect of yoghurt and mint to a hot, spicy taste of the East in chilli pepper sauces. Out of season, frozen French or runner beans, either your own produce or ones you have bought, are a quick and easy substitute.

When you are cooking dried beans of any kind for another dish, take the opportunity to prepare more than you need. Then you will have them at your fingertips, ready to assemble as salads and starters in moments. Cooked dried beans mean endless variety. Combine them with fresh vegetables, fruit, cheese, canned or smoked fish, cold meats, pasta, what you will. These recipes, a selection of classic and country dishes from all over the world, point the way to some of the possibilities.

COURGETTE AND BEAN SALAD

These two vegetables make a well-balanced mixed green salad.

    325 g (12 oz) tiny courgettes
    325 g (12 oz) very young whole French beans
    15 ml (1 tablespoon) lemon juice
    2 bananas, peeled and sliced
    2 spring onions, trimmed and sliced

For the Yoghurt Dressing
    75 ml (3 fl. oz) natural yoghurt, chilled
    15 ml (1 tablespoon) fresh chopped mint leaves
    1 large clove garlic, peeled and crushed
    salt and freshly-ground black pepper
    5 ml (1 teaspoon) clear honey

Trim the courgettes and cut them slantwise into chunks. Trim the French beans. Blanch the vegetables in boiling, salted water for about 5 minutes. Drain and cool them. Sprinkle the lemon juice on the bananas and mix them with the courgettes, beans and spring onions.

Blend the yoghurt dressing ingredients well together, and toss the salad to coat it thoroughly. Serve well chilled.
Serves 4–6

FRENCH BEAN AND YOGHURT SALAD

As cool as a cucumber on a summer day, this Iranian salad can be served as a first course, or an accompaniment to a spicy main dish.

> 550 g (1¼ lb) young whole French beans, cooked
> 1 small onion, peeled and finely chopped
> 15 ml (1 tablespoon) lemon juice
> salt and freshly-ground black pepper
> 1 clove garlic, peeled and crushed
> 15 ml (1 tablespoon) fresh chopped mint leaves
> 300 ml (½ pint) natural yoghurt, chilled

Put the beans, onion and lemon juice in a salad bowl and season well with salt and pepper. Stir the garlic and mint into the yoghurt and pour on the salad. Gently toss it to mix in the dressing. Serve well chilled.
Serves 4

PINK AND GREEN SALAD

For a straight-from-the-cupboard meal, use canned prawns.

> 1 small lettuce heart, shredded
> 4 tomatoes, skinned and quartered
> 175 g (6 oz) young whole French beans, cooked
> 8 stuffed olives, halved
> 1 × 50-g (2-oz) can anchovy fillets, drained and halved
> 100 g (4 oz) peeled prawns
> 2 hard-boiled eggs, shelled and sliced

For the Dressing
60 ml (4 tablespoons) salad oil
30 ml (2 tablespoons) lemon juice
salt and freshly-ground black pepper
pinch of sugar
a little mustard powder

Divide the lettuce between four serving bowls or plates. Mix the tomatoes, beans, olives, anchovy fillets and prawns together. Put the salad dressing ingredients into a screw-topped jar and shake thoroughly. Pour the dressing over the salad and toss gently. Divide the salad between the bowls and decorate with egg slices.
Serves 4

RUNNER BEANS WITH MUSHROOMS

A hint of the Balkans in this soured cream dressing spiced with paprika.

325 g (12 oz) runner beans or French beans, cooked
100 g (4 oz) button mushrooms, wiped and sliced
2 hard-boiled eggs, shelled and sliced

For the Dressing
125 ml (scant $\frac{1}{4}$ pint) fresh soured cream
30 ml (2 tablespoons) olive oil
15 ml (1 tablespoon) garlic vinegar
salt and freshly-ground black pepper
1.5 ml ($\frac{1}{4}$ teaspoon) paprika
1.5 ml ($\frac{1}{4}$ teaspoon) sugar

Put the beans and mushrooms into a bowl. Put the salad dressing ingredients into another bowl and beat or whisk them thoroughly. Pour the dressing over the vegetables and toss gently. Cover and leave in the refrigerator for about 30 minutes to chill. Serve garnished with the hard-boiled egg slices.
Serves 4

SALADE NIÇOISE

French beans are a traditional ingredient in this regional salad, which can be served as a first course or, with plenty of hot, crusty bread, as a light lunch dish.

  1 cos lettuce, torn into strips
  225 g (8 oz) young whole French beans, cooked and cut into
     4-cm (1½-in) chunks
  ½ small cucumber, diced
  1 small green pepper, trimmed and thinly sliced
  1 small onion, peeled and cut into thin rings
  3 tomatoes, skinned and quartered
  8 black olives
  1 × 175-g (6-oz) can tuna fish, drained and flaked
  1 × 50-g (2-oz) can anchovy fillets, drained and halved
  2 hard-boiled eggs, shelled and quartered

For the Dressing
  45 ml (3 tablespoons) salad oil
  25 ml (1½ tablespoons) white wine vinegar
  salt and freshly-ground black pepper
  2.5 ml (½ teaspoon) French mustard
  2.5 ml (½ teaspoon) caster sugar
  1 large clove garlic, peeled and crushed

Arrange the lettuce in a salad bowl. Put the prepared beans, cucumber, pepper, onion, tomatoes and olives into another bowl.

Put the dressing ingredients into a screw-topped jar and shake thoroughly. Pour the dressing over the prepared vegetables and toss gently. Add the tuna and anchovies, turning them carefully in the dressing. Spoon the salad on to the lettuce and top with the wedges of hard-boiled egg.
Serves 4

SCALLOP SALAD

A delightful summer lunch dish, or a perfect start to a dinner party.

  675 g (1½ lb) scallops, fresh or frozen
  6 large lettuce leaves

450 g (1 lb) young whole French beans, cooked
1 small onion, peeled and cut into thin rings
2 stalks celery, thinly sliced
1 canned pimento, drained and chopped

For the Marinade
30 ml (2 tablespoons) salad oil
60 ml (4 tablespoons) cider vinegar
5 ml (1 teaspoon) caster sugar
salt and freshly-ground black pepper
pinch of cayenne pepper

Wash the scallops, drop them into a pan of boiling salted water,
cover and simmer for 3–4 minutes. Drain and cool the scallops,
slice them and put them in a bowl. Beat the marinade ingredients together until blended, then pour over the scallops.
Cover and set aside for at least 1 hour.

Arrange the lettuce leaves on a plate, add the prepared
vegetables to the marinade with the scallops and toss gently.
Spoon the salad over the lettuce. Serve chilled.
Serves 4–6

SPINACH AND BEAN SALAD

Spinach salad is a favourite in Greece, here with the homely
addition of fresh green beans.

4 rashers bacon
225 g (8 oz) spinach, shredded
325 g (12 oz) young whole French beans, cooked

For the Dressing
90 ml (6 tablespoons) olive oil
30 ml (2 tablespoons) white wine vinegar
5 ml (1 teaspoon) lemon juice
2.5 ml ($\frac{1}{2}$ teaspoon) mustard powder
salt and freshly-ground black pepper
1.5 ml ($\frac{1}{4}$ teaspoon) sugar

Remove the rind from the bacon, chop the bacon into pieces.
Fry them over a low heat in a non-stick pan until crisp. Allow
to cool, then mix the bacon pieces with the spinach and beans.

Put the dressing ingredients into a screw-topped jar and shake thoroughly. Pour the dressing over the spinach mixture and toss gently.

Serve the salad as soon as you have 'dressed' it, or the spinach will wilt and discolour.

Serves 4

TOMATO AND BEAN SALAD

Choose the youngest, most tender green beans for this stunningly colourful salad.

    450 g (1 lb) firm tomatoes, thinly sliced
    450 g (1 lb) young whole French beans, cooked
    50 g (2 oz) Mozzarella cheese, cubed

    For the Dressing
    75 ml (5 tablespoons) salad oil
    30 ml (2 tablespoons) white wine vinegar
    salt and freshly-ground black pepper
    2.5 ml ($\frac{1}{2}$ teaspoon) French mustard
    2.5 ml ($\frac{1}{2}$ teaspoon) sugar
    1 clove garlic, peeled and crushed

Put the tomatoes and beans in a shallow serving dish. Put the dressing ingredients into a screw-topped jar and shake thoroughly. Pour the dressing over the vegetables. Gently turn the tomatoes and beans in the dressing, using two spoons and taking care not to break up the salad. Scatter the Mozzarella cubes on top, just before serving.

Serves 4

BROAD BEAN AND BACON SALAD

There's a special link between broad beans and bacon, a really good combination. Use ham instead if it's more convenient.

    4 rashers bacon
    450 g (1 lb) broad beans, cooked (shelled weight)
    4 spring onions, trimmed and sliced
    1 green pepper, trimmed and thinly sliced
    5 ml (1 teaspoon) fresh chopped chives

25 g (1 oz) walnuts, chopped

For the Dressing
30 ml (2 tablespoons) salad oil
15 ml (1 tablespoon) white wine vinegar
salt and freshly-ground black pepper
1.5 ml ($\frac{1}{4}$ teaspoon) caster sugar

Remove the rind from the bacon, chop the bacon into pieces.
Fry them over a low heat in a non-stick pan until crisp. Remove
the bacon with a draining spoon and set aside to cool.

Mix the broad beans, spring onions, pepper and chives together in a bowl. Put the dressing ingredients into a screw-
topped jar and shake thoroughly. Pour the dressing on to the
vegetables and toss gently. Just before serving, stir in the
bacon. Sprinkle with the chopped walnuts.
Serves 4

BROAD BEAN HORS D'OEUVRE

Broad beans combine extremely well with store-cupboard
'openers' to make a varied first course.

450 g (1 lb) broad beans, cooked (shelled weight)
15 ml (1 tablespoon) fresh chopped parsley
2 × 125-g (5-oz) cans sardines in olive oil, drained
4 hard-boiled eggs, shelled and sliced
8 black olives

For the Dressing
30 ml (2 tablespoons) salad oil
15 ml (1 tablespoon) white wine vinegar
2.5 ml ($\frac{1}{2}$ teaspoon) mustard powder
salt and freshly-ground black pepper
5 ml (1 teaspoon) top of the milk

Mix the broad beans and parsley together. Put the dressing
ingredients into a screw-topped jar and shake thoroughly.
Pour the dressing over the beans and toss gently. Arrange the
sardines in a wheel pattern or in rows on a serving dish, and
arrange the beans, egg slices and olives around them.
Serves 4

B.–C

WINTER SALAD

Chinese leaves give us the chance to make crisp green salads in winter, and canned or frozen beans give us plenty of variety.

   8 leaves from a Chinese cabbage
   225 g (8 oz) broad beans, cooked (use canned or frozen ones, drained or thawed)
   4 stalks celery, sliced
   1 avocado pear, peeled, stoned and diced
   100 g (4 oz) button mushrooms, wiped and sliced
   15 ml (1 tablespoon) fresh soured cream
   60 ml (4 tablespoons) mayonnaise
   freshly-ground black pepper
   15 ml (1 tablespoon) fresh chopped parsley

Arrange the cabbage leaves around a salad bowl. If they are very large, cut them into strips with scissors. Toss the broad beans, celery, avocado and mushrooms together. Stir the soured cream into the mayonnaise and season well with pepper. Toss the vegetables in the dressing. Pile the salad into the bowl, sprinkle with parsley and serve well chilled.
Serves 4

BEAN SPROUT AND MUSHROOM SALAD

An attractive salad with strong colour contrasts.

   6 spring onions, trimmed and sliced
   2 stalks celery, sliced
   100 g (4 oz) button mushrooms, wiped and sliced
   225 g (8 oz) fresh bean sprouts (or canned ones, drained and rinsed)
   4 hard-boiled eggs, shelled and quartered

   For the Dressing
   1 clove garlic, peeled and halved
   45 ml (3 tablespoons) salad oil
   20 ml (1½ tablespoons) white wine vinegar
   2.5 ml (½ teaspoon) caster sugar
   5 ml (1 teaspoon) soya sauce
   salt and freshly-ground black pepper

Put the garlic clove into a screw-topped jar, add the remaining dressing ingredients and shake thoroughly. Leave the garlic to infuse while you prepare the vegetables, then remove it.

About 15 minutes before you are ready to serve the salad, mix together the prepared spring onions, celery and mushrooms in a salad bowl, pour on the dressing and toss the vegetables gently. Just before serving, toss in the bean sprouts and mix them thoroughly with the other vegetables. Arrange the egg wedges in a wheel pattern on top.

Serves 4

MANGE-TOUT PEA SALAD

In this Chinese-style salad, the pods are cooked so fleetingly that they taste as good as fresh.

15 ml (1 tablespoon) vegetable oil
1 clove garlic, peeled and finely chopped
2.5 ml ($\frac{1}{2}$ teaspoon) salt
2 stalks celery, thinly sliced
325 g (12 oz) mange-tout peas
100 g (4 oz) fresh bean sprouts (or canned ones, drained and rinsed)
60 ml (4 tablespoons) chicken stock
5 ml (1 teaspoon) sugar
5 ml (1 teaspoon) white wine vinegar
5 ml (1 teaspoon) soya sauce

Heat the oil in a heavy-based pan until it is hot but not smoking. Add the garlic and salt, then the celery and stir-fry over a medium heat for 1 minute. Add the peas, stir for 1 minute more, then add the bean sprouts. Stir to coat with oil. Add the stock, sugar, vinegar and soya sauce mixed together, increase the heat and cook for 2 minutes. Remove the pan from the heat and cool.

Serve the salad well chilled, with soya sauce if liked.

Serves 4

BEAN AND PEA SALAD

Plan ahead for this mixed salad, and cook some extra dried
beans and peas when you are preparing other dishes. They
will keep for several days in the refrigerator.

> 100 g (4 oz) dried kidney beans, cooked
> 100 g (4 oz) dried chick peas, cooked
> 225 g (8 oz) runner beans, cooked
> 4 spring onions, trimmed and sliced

> *For the Dressing*
> 45 ml (3 tablespoons) salad oil
> 20 ml (1½ tablespoons) garlic vinegar
> salt and freshly-ground black pepper
> 1.5 ml (¼ teaspoon) sugar
> 2.5 ml (½ teaspoon) dried basil

Mix together the beans, chick peas, runner beans and onions.
Put the dressing ingredients into a screw-topped jar and shake
thoroughly. Pour the dressing on to the vegetables and toss
gently.
Serves 4

BEAN CURD SALAD

You can buy squares of bean curd, fresh or canned, in Oriental
grocers. As it readily absorbs other flavours, you can serve it
with any of your favourite salad dressings.

> 4 Chinese cabbage leaves
> 6 squares soft bean curd

> *For the Dressing*
> 2 spring onions, trimmed and chopped
> 7.5 ml (1½ teaspoons) soya sauce
> 5 ml (1 teaspoon) sesame oil
> 10 ml (2 teaspoons) clear honey
> salt and freshly-ground black pepper
> 15 ml (1 tablespoon) fresh chopped celery leaves, if available

Wash and shred the Chinese leaves and arrange them on four
individual serving dishes or plates. Wash and slice the bean

curd and arrange it on the leaves. Put the dressing ingredients into a screw-topped jar and shake thoroughly. Pour the dressing over the bean curd. Garnish with fresh chopped celery leaves, or fresh herbs.

Serves 4

BLACK-EYED BEAN SALAD

Beans and garlic make a robust partnership in this country salad.

225 g (8 oz) bacon pieces
225 g (8 oz) dried black-eyed beans, cooked
1 medium-sized onion, peeled and chopped
1 large tomato, thinly sliced

For the Dressing
45 ml (3 tablespoons) salad oil
20 ml (1½ tablespoons) garlic vinegar
1 clove garlic, peeled and crushed
salt and freshly-ground black pepper
1.5 ml (¼ teaspoon) sugar
2.5 ml (½ teaspoon) dried oregano

Remove the rinds from the bacon pieces, chop the bacon into chunks. Fry in a non-stick pan until crisp. Remove the bacon with a draining spoon and set aside to cool. Mix with the beans and onion.

Put the dressing ingredients into a screw-topped jar and shake thoroughly. Pour the dressing on to the salad and toss gently. Serve garnished with tomato slices.

Serves 4

CHEESE AND BEAN SALAD

Creamy soft bean seeds and crisp and crunchy shoots together demonstrate the vegetable's versatility.

1 × 215-g (7½-oz) can butter beans
1 large carrot, peeled and thinly sliced
1 green pepper, trimmed and thinly sliced
7.5 ml (1 heaped teaspoon) fresh chopped parsley or chives
12 stuffed olives, sliced
225 g (8 oz) fresh bean sprouts (or canned ones, drained and rinsed)
100 g (4 oz) Edam cheese, cut into small cubes

For the Honey Dressing
45 ml (3 tablespoons) salad oil
15 ml (1 tablespoon) cider vinegar
2.5 ml (½ teaspoon) lemon juice
salt and freshly-ground black pepper
15 ml (1 tablespoon) clear honey

Thoroughly drain the butter beans and put them into a bowl with the prepared carrot, green pepper, parsley and stuffed olives. Put the dressing ingredients into a screw-topped jar and shake thoroughly. Pour the dressing on to the salad ingredients and toss gently. Just before serving, toss in the bean sprouts and stir to coat them in the dressing. Sprinkle the cheese cubes on top.
Serves 4

CHICK PEA SALAD

Chick peas, roughly the size and shape of small hazelnuts, make a good first-course salad, served with plenty of crusty bread.

325 g (12 oz) dried chick peas, soaked
pinch of bicarbonate of soda
salt
15 ml (1 tablespoon) fresh chopped parsley
1 small onion, peeled and cut into thin rings

For the Dressing
75 ml (5 tablespoons) olive oil
30 ml (2 tablespoons) white wine vinegar
2 large cloves garlic, crushed
salt and freshly-ground black pepper

Cook the chick peas in boiling water with the bicarbonate of soda, adding salt just before the peas are cooked – about 3 hours. Drain and cool the peas.

Put the dressing ingredients into a screw-topped jar and shake thoroughly. Put the peas in a serving dish, pour the dressing over and toss gently. Garnish with the parsley and onion rings.
Serves 4

CHICK PEAS WITH GARLIC BUTTER

It couldn't be simpler, but it's a delicious and highly original way to start a meal.

325 g (12 oz) dried chick peas, soaked
pinch of bicarbonate of soda
salt
5 ml (1 teaspoon) lemon juice
3 cloves garlic, peeled and crushed
30 ml (2 tablespoons) fresh chopped parsley
75 g (3 oz) unsalted butter
freshly-ground black pepper

Cook the chick peas in boiling water with the bicarbonate of soda, adding salt just before the peas are cooked – about 3 hours. Drain and cool the peas.

Beat the lemon juice, garlic and parsley into the butter, shape it into a roll and wrap it in foil. Return to the refrigerator to chill.

Turn the peas into a heated serving dish. Cut the butter into round pats and scatter them over the peas. Season with black pepper. Serve with plenty of French bread to soak up the butter.

Haricot beans are good served in this way, too.
Serves 4

SPICED CHICK PEA SALAD

Impressively 'different' for a dinner party, a salad full of
variety.

> 325 g (12 oz) dried chick peas, soaked
> pinch of bicarbonate of soda
> salt
> 5 ml (1 teaspoon) ground cumin
> 1 large onion, peeled and chopped
> 2 large cloves garlic, peeled and crushed
> 3 large firm tomatoes, skinned and quartered
> 12 black olives
> salt and freshly-ground black pepper
> 15 ml (1 tablespoon) fresh chopped mint leaves
> 15 ml (1 tablespoon) fresh chopped coriander leaves (or use
>   parsley)
> a few cumin seeds
> 45 ml (3 tablespoons) lemon juice
> 60 ml (4 tablespoons) olive oil
> 175 g (6 oz) feta cheese, crumbled (or use Wensleydale or
>   goat's milk cheese)

Cook the chick peas in boiling water with the bicarbonate of
soda. Add the salt and ground cumin just before the end of
cooking time – about 3 hours. Drain and cool the peas.

Mix them in a salad bowl with the garlic, tomatoes and
olives. Season well with salt and pepper, the herbs and cumin
seeds, and pour on the lemon juice and oil. Toss the salad with
two spoons to 'dress' it thoroughly. Scatter the cheese on top.
Serves 4–6

HARICOT BEAN AND TOMATO SALAD

Lovely in the spring, when the first, rather pale, tomatoes are
in the shops.

> 225 g (8 oz) dried haricot beans, soaked
> salt
> 325 g (12 oz) firm tomatoes, skinned and sliced
> 2 spring onions, trimmed and sliced

For the Dressing
45 ml (3 tablespoons) fresh soured cream
15 ml (1 tablespoon) tarragon vinegar
2.5 ml (½ teaspoon) fresh chopped tarragon, if available
salt and freshly-ground black pepper

Cook the beans in boiling water until they are just tender,
adding salt just before the end of the cooking time – about 1
hour. Drain and cool the beans.

Mix the beans, tomatoes and spring onions together in a
salad bowl, taking care not to break up the tomatoes. Thoroughly blend all the dressing ingredients together, and adjust the
seasoning if necessary. Stir the dressing gently into the salad.
Serves 4

HARICOT BEAN AND TUNA SALAD

A favourite *antipasto* in Italian restaurants, a salad that is
cheatingly simple to prepare.

225 g (8 oz) dried white haricot beans, soaked
salt
1 medium-sized onion, peeled and chopped
1 × 175-g (6-oz) can tuna fish, drained
8 black olives

For the Dressing
30 ml (2 tablespoons) olive oil
15 ml (1 tablespoon) white wine vinegar
1 clove garlic, crushed
salt and freshly-ground black pepper
5 ml (1 teaspoon) dried oregano

Cook the beans in boiling water until they are just tender,
adding salt just before the end of the cooking time – about 1
hour. Drain and cool the beans. Mix the beans with the onion.

Put the dressing ingredients into a screw-topped jar and
shake thoroughly. Pour the dressing over the beans and stir
gently. Carefully fold in the tuna fish. Garnish with olives.
Serves 4

HUMMUS

One of the delights of eating in a Middle-Eastern restaurant is this traditional salad 'starter' of ground chick peas and olive oil.

    225 g (8 oz) dried chick peas, soaked
    pinch of bicarbonate of soda
    salt
    5 ml (1 teaspoon) ground cumin
    60 ml (4 tablespoons) olive oil
    60 ml (4 tablespoons) lemon juice
    2 large cloves garlic, peeled and crushed
    freshly-ground black pepper
    15 ml (1 tablespoon) fresh chopped parsley

Cook the chick peas in boiling water with a pinch of bicarbonate of soda. Add the salt and ground cumin just before the end of the cooking time – about 3 hours. Put the cooked chick peas with a very little of the water into a blender and liquidize to a purée. Pour on the olive oil and lemon juice, add the garlic and pepper and blend again to a smooth paste. Add a little more of the cooking liquor if necessary. Or rub the peas through a sieve and beat in the other ingredients. Sprinkle with the parsley and serve with hot pitta bread, if available.

You can, if you like, reserve a few chick peas before puréeing the mixture and use them as a garnish.

Serves 4

HUMMUS WITH SESAME PASTE

This version, with sesame paste (available from health food shops) is more aromatic.

    225 g (8 oz) dried chick peas, soaked
    pinch of bicarbonate of soda
    salt
    225 g (8 oz) *tahina* (sesame seed paste)
    60 ml (4 tablespoons) lemon juice
    2 large cloves garlic, peeled and crushed
    15 ml (1 tablespoon) fresh chopped parsley

Cook the chick peas in boiling water with a pinch of bicarbonate of soda, adding salt just before the end of the cooking time – about 3 hours. Liquidize or sieve them with a little of the cooking water to make a smooth paste. Blend or beat in the *tahina*, lemon juice and garlic, until you have a thin paste. Garnish the *hummus* with parsley.

Each person takes a spoonful of the salad on to his plate, and scoops it up with hot pitta bread. French bread is probably the best substitute if this is not available.
Serves 4–6

STUFFED TOMATOES

A lovely first course with plenty of eye appeal.

8 large firm tomatoes
1 × 90-g (3½-oz) can tuna fish
100 g (4 oz) dried haricot beans, cooked
6 stuffed olives, chopped
30 ml (2 tablespoons) mayonnaise
salt and freshly-ground black pepper
a few watercress sprigs or parsley sprigs

Cut the tomatoes in half horizontally, inserting the knife point through to the centre first one way, then the other, to make a zig-zag edge. Scoop out the seeds. (Use them for soup or a casserole).

Drain and flake the tuna fish. Mix it with the beans, olives and mayonnaise, taking care not to break the fish too much, and season well with salt and pepper. Spoon the filling into the tomatoes and garnish them with watercress or parsley sprigs.
Serves 4

CHICKEN AND BEAN SALAD

A way of stretching yesterday's chicken that children will enjoy
more than yesterday's chicken.

    4 large lettuce leaves
    1 × 447-g (15¾-oz) can baked beans
    45 ml (3 tablespoons) mayonnaise
    15 ml (1 tablespoon) white wine vinegar
    salt and freshly-ground black pepper
    325 g (12 oz) cooked chicken, diced
    6 spring onions, trimmed and sliced
    3 stalks celery, sliced
    1 dessert apple, cored and chopped
    15 ml (1 tablespoon) lemon juice
    fresh chopped parsley

Arrange the lettuce leaves on a serving dish. Drain the sauce
from the baked beans into a bowl and thoroughly mix in the
mayonnaise and vinegar, and season with salt and pepper. Fold
in the chopped chicken. Spoon the chicken salad into a ring
around the outside of the serving dish.

    Mix together the beans, spring onions, celery, apple and
lemon juice and pile the salad into the centre. Sprinkle with a
little chopped parsley to garnish.

Serves 4

SUNDANCE SLAW

Canned baked beans have enough ready-made tomato sauce to
spare for the salad vegetables.

    1 × 447-g (15¾-oz) can baked beans in tomato sauce
    60 ml (4 tablespoons) mayonnaise
    salt and freshly-ground black pepper
    a few drops of Worcestershire sauce
    225 g (8 oz) firm white cabbage, shredded
    1 large carrot, peeled and grated
    ½ cucumber, diced
    2 spring onions, trimmed and sliced

Tip the baked beans into a bowl and stir in the mayonnaise, salt and pepper and Worcestershire sauce. Fold in the prepared vegetables and mix thoroughly. Serve chilled.
Serves 4–6

Fresh from the garden or straight from the kitchen shelves, beans are a wonderfully versatile accompaniment to meat, fish and other vegetables.

From the basic ways to cook them described in Chapter 3, we come to a batch of recipes in which the beans blend with herb, cream, spiced and tomato sauces, with fruit and vegetable garnishes and with rice and pasta for double-interest dishes.

In these days of casual cooking and relaxed entertaining, no dish is suitable only as a starter, accompaniment to the main course, or as a main course itself. This book has been divided into such sections only as a general guide – and, sure as eggs, you'll find recipes here that you'll want to serve as a whole, delicious main dish.

BROAD BEANS IN CREAM SAUCE

A good 'party' way to dress fresh beans.

450 g (1 lb) broad beans (shelled weight)
salt
1 egg yolk
150 ml ($\frac{1}{4}$ pint) single cream
freshly-ground black pepper
15 ml (1 tablespoon) fresh chopped parsley

Cook the beans in boiling, salted water until they are just tender – about 10–12 minutes. Drain them well and return them to the pan.

Beat the egg yolk into the cream and season with pepper. Stir the sauce into the beans, using a wooden spoon. Cook over a very low heat for 2 minutes, without boiling. Just before serving, stir in the parsley.

Serves 4

WHOLE BROAD BEANS WITH PARSLEY SAUCE

450 g (1 lb) very small whole broad beans, washed and
    trimmed
salt
25 g (1 oz) butter
25 g (1 oz) flour
300 ml (½ pint) milk
freshly-ground black pepper
pinch of nutmeg
15 ml (1 tablespoon) double cream
30 ml (2 tablespoons) fresh chopped parsley

Cook the beans in boiling, salted water until they are tender –
about 10–12 minutes. Drain them well.

To make the sauce, melt the butter in a small pan, stir in the
flour and cook until it forms a ball. Gradually pour on the
milk, stirring, and bring to the boil. Simmer the sauce for 3
minutes, season with salt, pepper and nutmeg, and stir in the
cream and chopped parsley. Toss the drained, cooked beans in
the sauce.
Serves 4

FRENCH BEANS
In these recipes for fresh whole French beans, you can substitute frozen beans, cooking them until they are just tender, or
very young runner beans.

FRENCH BEANS WITH APPLES

450 g (1 lb) young whole French beans, washed and trimmed
salt
50 g (2 oz) butter
1 medium-sized onion, peeled and sliced
2 large cooking apples, peeled, cored and chopped
15 ml (1 tablespoon) lemon juice

Cook the beans in boiling, salted water until they are just
tender – about 12–15 minutes. Drain them in a colander,
refresh them by running cold water through them. Drain them
well.

Meanwhile, melt the butter in a pan and fry the onion and
apples for 7–8 minutes over a medium heat. Stir in the lemon
juice and the beans and reheat gently, stirring to glaze the beans.
Serves 4

FRENCH BEANS WITH BACON

450 g (1 lb) young whole French beans, washed and trimmed
salt
50 g (2 oz) butter
1 large onion, peeled and thinly sliced
1 clove garlic, peeled and crushed
4 rashers bacon, de-rinded and chopped
25 g (1 oz) blanched almonds
freshly-ground black pepper

Cook the beans in boiling, salted water until just tender – about
12–15 minutes. Drain them in a colander, refresh them by
running cold water through them. Drain them well.

Melt the butter in a pan and fry the onion, garlic, bacon and
almonds over a medium heat for 5 minutes. Stir in the beans,
season them well and stir them over a low heat until they are
glazed and heated through.
Serves 4

FRENCH BEANS IN SOURED CREAM SAUCE

450 g (1 lb) young whole French beans, washed and trimmed
salt
30 ml (2 tablespoons) vegetable oil
2 medium-sized onions, peeled and finely chopped
15 ml (1 tablespoon) tomato purée
15 ml (1 tablespoon) paprika
150 ml ($\frac{1}{4}$ pint) fresh soured cream
freshly-ground black pepper
15 ml (1 tablespoon) fresh chopped parsley

Cook the beans until just tender in boiling, salted water – about
12–15 minutes. Drain them in a colander, refresh them by
running cold water through them. Drain them well.

Heat the oil in a pan and fry the onions over a medium heat

for 4–5 minutes, without allowing them to brown. Stir in the tomato purée, paprika and soured cream, and season with salt and pepper. Slowly heat the sauce, stir in the beans and heat them gently without letting the sauce boil. Garnish with the parsley before serving.
Serves 4

ITALIAN-STYLE BEANS

1 kg (2¼ lb) young whole French beans, washed and trimmed
salt
75 ml (5 tablespoons) olive oil
2 cloves garlic, peeled and halved
1 × 375-g (14-oz) can peeled tomatoes
2.5 ml (½ teaspoon) dried basil
freshly-ground black pepper

Cook the beans in boiling, salted water until they are tender – about 12–15 minutes. Drain them in a colander, refresh them by running cold water through them. Drain them well.

Heat the oil in a pan, fry the garlic until it is brown, then remove it. Add the tomatoes and their juice and the basil to the garlic-flavoured oil and season with salt and pepper. Stir well. Stir in the beans and simmer for 10–15 minutes, until the sauce is thick. Taste and adjust seasoning.
Serves 6–8

BEAN SPROUTS PROVENÇALE

Serve with any 'dry' meat dish, such as grilled chicken, steak or chops.

30 ml (2 tablespoons) vegetable oil
2 large onions, peeled and sliced
1 clove garlic, peeled and crushed
1 × 375-g (14-oz) can peeled tomatoes
2.5 ml (½ teaspoon) dried oregano
salt and freshly-ground black pepper
325 g (12 oz) fresh bean sprouts (or canned ones, drained and rinsed)
5 ml (1 teaspoon) fresh chopped parsley

Heat the oil in a pan and fry the onions and garlic over a medium heat for 4–5 minutes. Tip in the contents of the can of tomatoes, add the oregano and season well with salt and pepper. Stir well, then add the bean sprouts, stirring carefully to avoid breaking them up.

Bring slowly to the boil, reduce the heat and simmer for 10 minutes. Sprinkle with the parsley before serving.

Serves 4

BEAN SPROUTS AND PEPPERS

  45 ml (3 tablespoons) vegetable oil
  5 ml (1 teaspoon) salt
  2.5-cm (1-in) piece fresh ginger, peeled and very thinly sliced
  550 g (1¼ lb) fresh bean sprouts (or canned ones, drained and rinsed)
  2 green peppers, trimmed and thinly sliced
  30 ml (2 tablespoons) dry sherry
  5 ml (1 teaspoon) soya sauce

Heat a heavy-based frying-pan and pour in the oil. When it is almost smoking, add the salt and ginger and, a little at a time, the bean sprouts and peppers. Stir-fry over a high heat for 2 minutes, reduce the heat to medium and pour in the sherry and soya sauce. Stir-fry for 2 minutes, until the liquid has been absorbed.

Serves 6

GREEN PEA PURÉE

Many people maintain that this is the most delicious way of all to serve fresh green peas. It is a classic French dish, known as Purée Clamart.

  450 g (1 lb) fresh green peas (shelled weight)
  3 shallots, if available, or 1 small onion, peeled and chopped
  50 g (2 oz) butter
  60 ml (4 tablespoons) chicken stock, or water and stock cube
  salt and freshly-ground black pepper
  a pinch of sugar
  5 ml (1 teaspoon) fresh chopped parsley

Put the peas, shallots, butter, stock, seasonings and sugar in a
pan and bring to the boil. Cover and simmer for about 10–12
minutes, until the peas are soft and most of the liquid has been
absorbed. Liquidize in a blender and return the purée to the
pan. If the purée is runny, drive off the liquid by cooking with
the pan uncovered, over a medium heat. Taste and adjust
seasoning if necessary. Garnish with the chopped parsley.
Serves 4

PEAS IN CREAM SAUCE

450 g (1 lb) fresh green peas (shelled weight)
1 mint sprig
5 ml (1 teaspoon) sugar
salt
25 g (1 oz) butter
1 small onion, peeled and finely chopped
1 clove garlic, peeled and crushed
15 g (½ oz) flour
150 ml (¼ pint) single cream
freshly-ground black pepper
5 ml (1 teaspoon) fresh chopped mint leaves

Cook the peas in boiling water with the mint sprig, sugar and
salt until they are tender – about 10–12 minutes. Drain them
in a colander and discard the mint.

Melt the butter in a pan and fry the onion and garlic over a
medium heat for 4–5 minutes, without allowing the onion to
brown. Stir in the flour and gradually pour on the cream, stirring. Season with salt and pepper, stir in the peas and heat
gently. Garnish with the chopped mint before serving.
Serves 4

PEA SOUFFLÉ

For the highest praise of all, serve this super dinner party
soufflé to accompany the main dish or as a separate course.

    75 g (3 oz) butter
    50 g (2 oz) flour
    300 ml (½ pint) milk
    salt and freshly-ground black pepper
    4 eggs, separated
    300 ml (½ pint) pea purée (see page 82)
    100 g (4 oz) ham, finely chopped

Grease a 1.75-litre (2-pint) soufflé dish. Melt the butter in a
small pan, stir in the flour and cook until it forms a ball.
Gradually pour on the milk, stirring, and bring to the boil.
Simmer, still stirring, until the sauce thickens. Season with
salt and pepper and leave to cool slightly. Beat in the egg yolks,
then the pea purée and the ham.

In a clean, dry bowl whisk the egg whites to firm dry peaks.
Fold them very lightly into the sauce mixture and turn into
the greased dish. Bake in the oven preheated to 200°C (400°F),
Gas 6, for 40–45 minutes, until the soufflé is well risen and
golden brown. Serve at once.
Serves 4–6

PEAS WITH BABY TURNIPS

    450 g (1 lb) baby white turnips, trimmed, peeled and diced
    150 ml (¼ pint) water, boiling
    50 g (2 oz) butter
    1 fresh marjoram sprig
    salt and freshly-ground black pepper
    2.5 ml (½ teaspoon) sugar
    675 g (1½ lb) fresh green peas (shelled weight)
    60 ml (4 tablespoons) double cream

Put the turnips into a pan with the boiling water and half the
butter. Add the marjoram, salt, pepper and sugar and bring to
the boil. Simmer, uncovered, for 5 minutes. Add the remaining

butter and the peas, bring back to the boil and simmer, still
without covering the pan, for a further 10–12 minutes, until
the peas are just tender. Stir in the cream and serve sprinkled
with more black pepper.
Serves 6

PEAS WITH HAM

450 g (1 lb) fresh green peas (shelled weight)
1 mint sprig
5 ml (1 teaspoon) sugar
salt
25 g (1 oz) butter
1 medium-sized onion, peeled and sliced
100 g (4 oz) ham, chopped
freshly-ground black pepper
a good pinch ground allspice

Cook the peas in boiling water with the mint sprig, sugar and
salt until they are tender – about 10–12 minutes. Drain them
in a colander and discard the mint.

Melt the butter in a pan, fry the onion for 4–5 minutes over
a medium heat until it is transparent, then stir in the ham.
Season with pepper and allspice to taste, stir in the peas, and
heat gently.
Serves 4

PETITS POIS SIMMERED WITH LETTUCE

The classic French way to cook tender young green peas is
with the heart of a lettuce, so that the peas can cook in the
moisture drawn off from the leaves.

1 kg (2¼ lb) small green peas
75 g (3 oz) butter
60 ml (4 tablespoons) water
2 shallots, finely chopped
1 medium-sized lettuce heart, shredded
10 ml (2 teaspoons) sugar
salt

Shell the peas and wash them in a bowl of cold water. Pick out any damaged ones. Choose a pan with a tightly-fitting lid. Melt the butter and add the water. Add the peas, shallots, lettuce, sugar and a little salt to taste. Cover the pan and shake it well. Cook over a medium heat for about 10 minutes, shaking it occasionally. Taste to make sure that the peas are tender. Remove the lid from the pan and continue cooking for a further 2 minutes, or until the excess moisture has evaporated. Serve immediately.

Serves 4–6

PEAS WITH ONIONS

A little onion brings out the flavour in peas. More than a little makes an interesting combination.

450 g (1 lb) fresh green peas (shelled weight)
1 mint sprig
5 ml (1 teaspoon) sugar
salt
50 g (2 oz) butter
2 large onions, peeled and sliced
6 spring onions, trimmed and sliced
freshly-ground black pepper
5 ml (1 teaspoon) fresh chopped chives

Cook the peas in boiling water with the mint sprig, sugar and salt until they are tender – about 10–12 minutes. Drain them in a colander and discard the mint.

Melt the butter in a pan and fry the onions and spring onions over a medium heat for 4–5 minutes, until they are transparent. Stir in the peas and season with salt and pepper. Stir them in the butter to glaze and heat them. Garnish with chopped chives before serving.

Serves 4

DRIED BEANS

Remember that you can easily substitute other pulses for the ones suggested here, so long as you adjust the cooking times. And in many of these dishes you can use pre-cooked beans or peas, or canned ones, to cut down the preparation time.

BUTTER BEANS AND CELERY

225 g (8 oz) dried butter beans, soaked
25 g (1 oz) butter
1 medium-sized onion, peeled and sliced
salt and freshly-ground black pepper
2.5 ml ($\frac{1}{2}$ teaspoon) celery seeds
1 × 400-g (15-oz) can celery hearts, drained
15 ml (1 tablespoon) fresh chopped parsley

Drain the butter beans and cook them in boiling water until they are just tender – about 1–1$\frac{1}{2}$ hours.

Melt the butter in a pan and fry the onion over a medium heat for 4–5 minutes, until it is transparent. Stir in salt, pepper, celery seeds, the celery hearts and the drained beans, and allow them to heat through.

Garnish with the chopped parsley before serving.
Serves 4

BUTTER BEANS DAIRY-STYLE

225 g (8 oz) dried butter beans, soaked
1 small onion, peeled and sliced
1 stalk celery, sliced
1 bay leaf
25 g (1 oz) butter
25 g (1 oz) flour
250 ml (scant $\frac{1}{2}$ pint) milk
30 ml (2 tablespoons) double cream
15 ml (1 tablespoon) fresh chopped parsley
salt and freshly-ground black pepper

Drain the butter beans and cook them in boiling water with the onion, celery and bay leaf until they are just tender – about 1–1$\frac{1}{2}$ hours. Remove the bay leaf, drain the beans and reserve the liquor.

Melt the butter in a small pan, stir in the flour and cook until it forms a ball. Gradually pour on the milk, stirring, and bring to the boil. Simmer for 3 minutes. Stir in the bean mixture, the cream and parsley, and season with salt and pepper. Add a little of the cooking liquid if necessary to make a smooth pouring sauce.

Serves 4

DHAL

A simplified lentil curry to accompany meat or vegetable dishes.

    225 g (8 oz) lentils, washed
    825 ml (1½ pints) water, boiling
    1 bay leaf
    45 ml (3 tablespoons) vegetable oil
    2 large onions, peeled and chopped
    1 clove garlic, peeled and crushed
    10 ml (2 teaspoons) curry powder
    salt
    325 g (12 oz) tomatoes, skinned and chopped

Cook the lentils in the boiling water with the bay leaf until they are soft and have absorbed most of the liquid – about 1 hour. Remove the bay leaf. If the mixture is still runny, cook for a few minutes in the uncovered pan.

    Meanwhile, heat the oil in a pan and fry the onions and garlic over a medium heat until they are golden brown – about 7 minutes. Stir in the curry powder and salt and cook for 1 minute before adding the tomatoes. Cook for a further 5 minutes. Beat this mixture into the cooked lentils. Taste and adjust the seasoning if needed.

Serves 4

FARMHOUSE BEANS

A good accompaniment to roast or grilled lamb.

    225 g (8 oz) dried butter beans, soaked
    100 g (4 oz) salt pork
    1 medium-sized onion, peeled and stuck with 4 cloves
    a few parsley stalks
    1 bay leaf
    40 g (1½ oz) butter

2 cloves garlic, peeled and crushed
15 ml (1 tablespoon) fresh chopped parsley
15 ml (1 tablespoon) lemon juice
salt and freshly-ground black pepper

Drain the butter beans and cook them in boiling water with the salt pork, the onion stuck with cloves, and the parsley and bay leaf tied together, until they are just tender – about 1–1½ hours. Skim the surface with a draining spoon to remove the scum. Drain the beans and reserve the liquor. Discard the onion and herbs. Cut the salt pork into small cubes and return to the pan with the beans. Reheat slowly.

Cream the butter and beat in the garlic, parsley, lemon juice, salt and pepper. Cut into pieces.

Turn the bean mixture into a heated serving dish and add the flavoured butter pieces. Toss until the beans are well coated.

Serves 4

HARICOT BEANS PROVENÇALE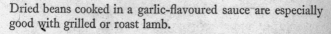

Dried beans cooked in a garlic-flavoured sauce are especially good with grilled or roast lamb.

30 ml (2 tablespoons) vegetable oil
1 large onion, peeled and finely chopped
2 cloves garlic, peeled and crushed
325 g (12 oz) dried white haricot beans, soaked and drained
1 × 375-g (14-oz) can peeled tomatoes
5 ml (1 teaspoon) dried oregano
salt and freshly-ground black pepper
15 ml (1 tablespoon) fresh chopped parsley

Heat the oil in a pan and fry the onion and garlic over a medium heat for 4–5 minutes. Add the beans, tomatoes and their juice, oregano, salt and pepper and bring slowly to the boil. Cover the pan and simmer for about 1–1½ hours, until the beans are tender. Garnish with the parsley before serving.

Serves 4–6

HOPPIN' JOHN

A traditional Southern American mixture of pulse and grain –
black-eyed beans with rice.

225 g (8 oz) dried black-eyed beans, soaked
600 ml (1 pint) water, boiling
225 g (8 oz) tomatoes, skinned
100 g (4 oz) brown rice
salt and freshly-ground black pepper
15 ml (1 tablespoon) fresh chopped parsley

Drain the beans and cook them in the boiling water for 1 hour.

Halve the tomatoes, scoop out and discard the seeds and
chop the flesh. Add to the pan with the rice and stir well.
Bring back to the boil, cover and simmer for 40 minutes, until
both the beans and rice are tender and the liquor has been
absorbed. Season well with salt and pepper, stir and leave to
'rest' on top of the stove for 5 minutes. Serve garnished with
the chopped parsley.
Serves 4

LENTILS WITH NOODLES

175 g (6 oz) brown lentils, washed
175 g (6 oz) fine noodles
salt
50 g (2 oz) butter
1 medium-sized onion, peeled and chopped
1 clove garlic, peeled and crushed
2.5 ml (½ teaspoon) ground coriander
freshly-ground black pepper
15 ml (1 tablespoon) fresh chopped parsley

Cook the lentils in boiling water until they are just tender –
¾–1 hour. Drain them and keep them warm. In a separate pan,
cook the noodles in boiling, salted water according to the
directions on the packet. Drain them and add them to the
lentils.

Meanwhile, melt half the butter in a small pan and fry the

onion and garlic over a medium heat for 4–5 minutes. Stir in the coriander, salt and pepper and continue frying for about 1 minute.

Grease and heat a serving dish and turn the lentils and noodles into it, then toss in the onion mixture, blending it in well. Garnish with the chopped parsley before serving.
Serves 4-6

MEXICAN CHILLI BEANS

30 ml (2 tablespoons) vegetable oil
2 medium-sized onions, peeled and sliced
1 large clove garlic, peeled and crushed
1 green pepper, trimmed and sliced
1 dried chilli pepper, trimmed and finely chopped (if available)
2.5 ml ($\frac{1}{2}$ teaspoon) chilli powder
1 × 375-g (14-oz) can peeled tomatoes
600 ml (1 pint) water
225 g (8 oz) dried red kidney beans, soaked
salt

Heat the oil in a pan, add the onions and garlic and fry for about 3 minutes over a medium heat. Add the green pepper and chilli pepper, if used, and the chilli powder and stir and fry for a further 2 minutes. Tip in all of the can of tomatoes and the water and add the drained beans. Bring to the boil, cover the pan and simmer for 1–1$\frac{1}{2}$ hours, until the beans are tender. Stir in salt to taste. If the dish is still runny, cook it in the uncovered pan over a high heat for a minute or so.
Serves 4

MOORS AND CHRISTIANS

A Cuban dish that is usually served simply, with fried eggs.

  225 g (8 oz) dried black beans, soaked and drained
  30 ml (2 tablespoons) vegetable oil
  1 medium-sized onion, peeled and chopped
  1 clove garlic, peeled and crushed
  1 green pepper, trimmed and chopped
  2 large tomatoes, skinned, seeded and chopped
  salt and freshly-ground black pepper
  175 g (6 oz) long-grain rice
  450 ml (¾ pint) water

Cook the beans in boiling water until they are barely tender –
about 2 hours. Drain them well.

  Meanwhile, heat the oil in a pan and fry the onion, garlic
and green pepper over a medium heat for 4–5 minutes. Add
the tomatoes to the pan and cook, stirring, until the mixture
thickens. Season with salt and pepper and stir in the beans,
rice and water. Stir well, cover the pan and simmer gently
until the rice is tender and the water has been absorbed – about
45 minutes. Taste and adjust seasoning if needed.
Serves 4–6

PAPRIKA BEANS

  225 g (8 oz) dried white haricot beans, soaked and drained
  1 small onion, peeled and stuck with 2 cloves
  1 bay leaf
  825 ml (1½ pints) water
  2 stalks celery, sliced
  1 medium-sized onion, peeled and sliced
  3 tomatoes, skinned and quartered
  15 ml (1 tablespoon) cider vinegar
  salt
  25 g (1 oz) butter
  25 g (1 oz) flour
  10 ml (2 teaspoons) paprika
  30 ml (2 tablespoons) natural yoghurt
  15 ml (1 tablespoon) fresh chopped parsley

Put the beans in a pan with the whole onion, bay leaf and water. Bring to the boil and simmer until the beans are almost tender – about 1 hour. Remove the onion and bay leaf.

Add the celery, onion, tomatoes and vinegar, and season with salt. Bring back to the boil and simmer for a further 30 minutes, until the vegetables are tender.

Beat the butter, flour and paprika together to form a paste and stir into the pan. Increase the heat and stir until the sauce has thickened. Turn into a heated serving dish and top with yoghurt and parsley.

Serves 4

PEASE PUDDING

The traditional way to cook this old English dish is wrapped in a cloth and suspended in a boiling pot – its function was to make a little boiled pork go a long way.

225 g (8 oz) dried split peas, soaked
1 small onion, peeled and halved
a bunch of fresh herbs, tied together
300 ml (½ pint) water
1 egg
salt and freshly-ground black pepper

Drain the peas and put them in a pan with the onion, herbs and water. Bring to the boil, cover the pan and simmer until the peas are tender – about 1 hour. Check during the cooking, stir occasionally, and add a little more boiling water if the peas are drying out before they are cooked. Beat the peas well to make a smooth purée – or liquidize them in a blender – and beat in the egg and seasoning. The purée should resemble a thick paste.

Either turn the purée into a greased and floured pudding cloth, tie it securely and boil it (preferably in meat stock) for 1 hour, or turn it into a shallow, greased ovenproof dish, level the surface and bake in the oven preheated to 180°C (350°F), Gas 4, for 30 minutes.

Serves 4

SPICED HARICOT BEANS

225 g (8 oz) dried haricot beans, soaked
50 g (2 oz) butter
1 medium-sized onion, peeled and chopped
2.5 ml ($\frac{1}{2}$ teaspoon) ground coriander
salt and freshly-ground black pepper
175 g (6 oz) small button mushrooms, wiped and trimmed
30 ml (2 tablespoons) double cream
15 ml (1 tablespoon) fresh chopped parsley

Drain the beans and cook them in boiling water until they are just tender – about 1–1$\frac{1}{2}$ hours. Drain them and keep them warm.

Melt the butter in a pan, fry the onion over a medium heat for about 2–3 minutes, then stir in the coriander, salt, pepper and mushrooms. Continue cooking, stirring occasionally, for about 3–4 minutes. Stir in the beans and cream. Garnish with a pinch of ground coriander and the parsley before serving.
Serves 4

SPLIT PEA PURÉE

Smooth and creamy, this purée makes a good alternative to potatoes.

325 g (12 oz) dried yellow split peas, soaked
825 ml (1$\frac{1}{2}$ pints) chicken stock, or water and stock cube
1 medium-sized onion, peeled and sliced
1 carrot, peeled and sliced
1 bay leaf
a few parsley stalks
freshly-ground black pepper
2.5 ml ($\frac{1}{2}$ teaspoon) ground coriander
salt
25 g (1 oz) butter, melted
15 ml (1 tablespoon) fresh chopped parsley

Drain the peas and put them in a pan with the chicken stock, onion, carrot and the bay leaf and parsley stalks tied together. Season with pepper and coriander and bring to the boil. Cover the pan and simmer for 1–1½ hours until the peas are mushy. Remove the bay leaf and parsley and add a little salt.

Purée the mixture in a blender or rub it through a sieve. Beat in the butter and gently reheat the purée over a very low heat. Taste and adjust the seasoning if necessary. Garnish with the parsley before serving.

Serves 6

SWEET AND SOUR BEANS

A mixed vegetable dish that goes well with grilled or roast meat, especially bacon and ham.

    225 g (8 oz) dried red kidney beans, soaked
    4 rashers streaky bacon, de-rinded and chopped
    1 medium-sized onion, peeled and chopped
    1 clove garlic, peeled and crushed
    2 large carrots, peeled and thinly sliced
    2 cooking apples, peeled, cored and sliced
    50 g (2 oz) sultanas
    15 ml (1 tablespoon) red wine vinegar
    15 ml (1 tablespoon) clear honey
    salt and freshly-ground black pepper

Drain the kidney beans and cook them in boiling water until they are just tender – about 1–1½ hours. Drain them well and reserve about 300 ml (½ pint) of the cooking liquor.

Meanwhile, fry the bacon in a non-stick pan over a medium heat until the fat runs. Add the onion and garlic and fry for 4–5 minutes. Add the carrots, apples and sultanas, stir well, and add the beans and reserved cooking liquor. Stir in the vinegar, honey, salt and pepper. Bring to the boil, cover the pan and simmer gently for about 15 minutes.

Serves 4–6

RICE WITH BEANS

Add a few cooked beans when you are cooking rice, to increase both the interest and protein.

150 ml ($\frac{1}{4}$ pint) chicken stock, or water and stock cube
3 cloves garlic, peeled and crushed
1 canned red pimento, drained and chopped
50 g (2 oz) ham, chopped
2 large tomatoes, skinned and chopped
15 ml (1 tablespoon) fresh chopped coriander leaves, if available (or use parsley)
salt and freshly-ground black pepper
325 g (12 oz) long-grain rice
100 g (4 oz) cooked red kidney beans (or canned ones, drained)
15 ml (1 tablespoon) fresh chopped parsley

Put the chicken stock in a pan with the garlic, pimento, ham, tomatoes and coriander and season with salt and pepper. Bring to the boil and simmer for about 4 minutes to allow the flavours to mellow. Stir in the rice and the cooked beans and add 600 ml (1 pint) water. Stir, then set over a low heat to simmer until the rice is tender and the water has been absorbed – about 30 minutes. Garnish with the chopped parsley.

Serves 6

7 Vegetable Dishes

Because beans are so full of protein, they represent an important as well as delicious part of a vegetable diet. If we choose not to eat meat or fish, whether it is on moral, aesthetic, economic or simply taste grounds, we can be grateful that beans go such a long way to making vegetable dishes a nutritious feast.

To form a completely balanced meal, beans should be served with a grain or dairy product in some form. Many of the following recipes, presenting beans in traditional country ways with pasta, have this taken well into account. Serve brown or white rice with the bean sauces, provide plenty of fresh wholemeal or crusty French bread with the casseroles, and you have the situation well in hand.

These recipes are for vegetable dishes, not truly vegetarian ones. Anyone who wishes to avoid eating animal derivatives will readily substitute vegetable fat for butter, vegetable for meat stock, soya milk for cow's milk, and so on.

BREAD SALAD

An Arabic country dish in which crisp bread croûtons contrast
well with mixed salad ingredients.

    4 thick slices day-old white bread
    40 g (1½ oz) butter
    1 clove garlic, peeled and halved
    1 large cucumber, trimmed and diced
    1 green pepper, trimmed and thinly sliced
    8 spring onions, trimmed and sliced
    1 lettuce heart, shredded
    225 g (8 oz) broad beans, cooked (shelled weight)
    15 ml (1 tablespoon) fresh chopped mint leaves
    15 ml (1 tablespoon) fresh finely chopped coriander leaves,
        if available (or use parsley)
    75 ml (5 tablespoons) olive oil
    30 ml (2 tablespoons) lemon juice
    salt and freshly-ground black pepper

Remove the crusts from the bread and cut the bread into cubes.
Melt the butter in a pan and fry the bread, tossing it once, until
it is golden brown and dry. Turn it on to crumpled kitchen
paper towels to drain thoroughly, and leave to cool.

Rub the garlic clove round the inside of a salad bowl and
discard it. Toss in the prepared cucumber, green pepper,
spring onions, lettuce and broad beans and stir in the herbs.
Just before you are ready to serve the salad, pour on the olive
oil and toss the salad carefully with two spoons, to coat the
vegetables thoroughly with the oil. Pour on the lemon juice,
season with salt and pepper and toss again. Stir in the bread
cubes last of all.
Serves 4

CHINESE MIXED VEGETABLES

A meal in itself, a dish of still crisp, still crunchy vegetables
stir-fried in oil.

    45 ml (3 tablespoons) vegetable or peanut oil
    1 clove garlic, peeled and crushed

2.5-cm (1-in) piece root ginger, peeled and sliced
salt and freshly-ground black pepper
2 stalks celery, thinly sliced
1 small cauliflower, trimmed and cut into florets
1 red pepper, trimmed and thinly sliced
100 g (4 oz) fresh bean sprouts
150 ml (¼ pint) chicken stock, or dry white wine
5 ml (1 teaspoon) clear honey
5 ml (1 teaspoon) soya sauce

Heat the oil in a large, heavy-bottomed frying-pan until it is very hot. Add the garlic, ginger, salt and pepper and fry over a high heat, stirring with a wooden spoon for 1 minute. Lower the heat to medium, add the celery and stir-fry for 1 minute. Add the cauliflower, then the red pepper and stir-fry for a further 2 minutes. Add the bean sprouts and stir-fry for 1 minute. Shake or stir the chicken stock, or wine, honey and soya sauce together, pour on to the vegetables and cover the pan. Cook for 3 minutes. Remove the lid and if there is still any liquor left cook uncovered for 1–2 minutes more. Serve very hot.
Serves 4

VEGETABLE ONE-POT

You just go on adding vegetables, until you have a steaming pot-full.

100 g (4 oz) dried butter beans, soaked
825 ml (1½ pints) water
100 g (4 oz) split peas, soaked
1 large onion, peeled and sliced
2 large carrots, peeled and sliced
1 small turnip, peeled and diced
2 courgettes, trimmed and thickly sliced
100 g (4 oz) broad beans (shelled weight)
2 large tomatoes, skinned and halved
salt and freshly-ground black pepper
2.5 ml (½ teaspoon) celery salt
15 g (½ oz) butter
15 g (½ oz) flour
5 ml (1 teaspoon) fresh chopped parsley

Drain the butter beans and put them in a large pan with the water. Bring to the boil, cover the pan and cook for 45 minutes. Drain the split peas, add them to the pan with the onion, carrots and turnip, bring back to the boil and cook, covered, for 30 minutes. Add the courgettes, broad beans and tomatoes, season with salt, pepper and celery salt and cook for a further 30 minutes. Check and add more boiling water if needed.

Work the butter and flour into a paste and stir it into the pan to thicken and glaze the stock. Cook for 5 minutes more. Garnish with the parsley before serving.

Serves 4

VEGETABLE CASSEROLE

1 large onion, peeled and sliced
2 large carrots, peeled and sliced
2 medium-sized potatoes, peeled and diced
1 medium-sized parsnip, peeled and diced
2 large tomatoes, skinned and quartered
225 g (8 oz) broad beans (shelled weight)
100 g (4 oz) French beans, topped, tailed and cut into 4-cm (1½-in) pieces
100 g (4 oz) fresh green peas (shelled weight)
salt and freshly-ground black pepper
600 ml (1 pint) chicken stock, or water and stock cube
25 g (1 oz) butter
25 g (1 oz) flour
300 ml (½ pint) dry cider
15 ml (1 tablespoon) fresh chopped parsley

Put all the prepared vegetables into a flameproof casserole, season well with salt and pepper and pour on the chicken stock. Bring to the boil, cover the casserole and transfer to the preheated oven. Cook at 180°C (350°F), Gas 4, for 1¼–1½ hours, until the potatoes and parsnips are tender. Remove the casserole from the oven and strain the stock from the vegetables. Reserve about 300 ml (½ pint). Keep the vegetables warm.

Melt the butter in a pan, stir in the flour and cook until it forms a ball. Gradually pour on the cider and reserved stock,

stirring, and bring to the boil. Stir until the sauce thickens, taste and season with salt and pepper. Pour the sauce over the vegetables in the casserole and stir gently with a wooden spoon, taking care not to break up the vegetables. Slowly reheat on top of the stove. Serve garnished with the parsley.
Serves 6

COCONUT BEANS

This West Indian dish is traditionally served with rice for a perfect balance of pulse and grain.

    225 g (8 oz) dried red kidney beans, soaked
    1 large onion, peeled and sliced
    1 clove garlic, peeled and crushed
    1 large carrot, peeled and sliced
    5 ml (1 teaspoon) dried thyme
    75 g (3 oz) coconut fat (from health food stores)
    salt and freshly-ground black pepper
    25 g (1 oz) desiccated coconut

Drain the beans and put them in a pan with 825 ml (1½ pints) water, the onion, garlic, carrot and thyme. Bring to the boil, cover the pan and cook for 1½ hours, until the beans are tender.

Cut the coconut fat into small pieces and gradually add them to the pan. Stir to blend thoroughly. Season with salt and plenty of pepper.

Time the cooking of long-grain rice so that it is ready at the same time as the beans. Serve the beans hot, as a sauce with the rice, and garnish with the coconut.
Serves 4

PINTO BEANS WITH BANANA RICE

325 g (12 oz) dried pinto beans, soaked
60 ml (4 tablespoons) vegetable oil
2 large onions, peeled and chopped
2 cloves garlic, peeled and crushed
1 × 375-g (14-oz) can peeled tomatoes, drained
1 bay leaf
salt and freshly-ground black pepper
a pinch of sugar
225 g (8 oz) long-grain rice
40 g (1½ oz) sultanas
25 g (1 oz) butter
2 small bananas, sliced
15 ml (1 tablespoon) fresh chopped parsley

Drain the beans and cook them in boiling water until they are
tender – about 1½–2 hours. Drain them well.

Meanwhile, heat the oil in a pan and fry the onions and
garlic over a medium heat for 4–5 minutes. Add the tomatoes,
bay leaf, salt, pepper and sugar and cook, stirring occasionally,
for 10 minutes. Stir in the beans and continue cooking for 5
minutes. Remove the bay leaf, and turn the beans on to a
heated serving dish.

Cook the rice in plenty of boiling, salted water until it is just
tender, about 20 minutes, strain it into a colander and return
it to the pan with the sultanas, butter and bananas.

Spoon the rice into a ring round the bean mixture and garnish with the parsley.

Serves 4–6

RED BEANS AND GOLDEN CORN

325 g (12 oz) dried red kidney beans, soaked
45 ml (3 tablespoons) vegetable oil
1 large onion, peeled and sliced
2 cloves garlic, peeled and crushed
4 stalks celery, sliced
1 red pepper, trimmed and sliced

325 g (12 oz) tomatoes, skinned and chopped
1 bay leaf
a few parsley stalks
salt and freshly-ground black pepper
1 × 200-g (7-oz) can sweetcorn kernels, drained
15 ml (1 tablespoon) fresh chopped parsley
15 ml (1 teaspoon) fresh chopped thyme leaves
75 g (3 oz) Gruyère cheese, cubed

Cook the drained beans in boiling water until they are tender – about 1–1½ hours. Drain them well.

Meanwhile heat the oil in a large pan and fry the onion and garlic over a medium heat for 4–5 minutes. Add the celery and red pepper and continue cooking, stirring occasionally, for about 10 minutes. Add the tomatoes, the bay leaf and parsley tied together and season with salt and pepper. Cover the pan and cook over a low heat for 30 minutes. Remove the parsley and bay leaf. Stir in the sweetcorn, beans, parsley, thyme and cheese, and leave over a low heat until the beans have heated through and the cheese begins to melt. Serve hot.

A green salad is a good accompaniment.
Serves 4–6

REVYTHIA CASSEROLE

I don't know what it is about this Greek Island dish that creates the illusion that it's brim-full of meat. But it fooled me.

350 g (12 oz) dried chick peas, soaked
a pinch of bicarbonate of soda
30 ml (2 tablespoons) olive oil
1 large onion, peeled and sliced
2 cloves garlic, peeled and crushed
2 stalks celery, thinly sliced
1 green pepper, trimmed and chopped
10 ml (2 teaspoons) fresh basil or 5 ml (1 teaspoon) dried basil
30 ml (2 tablespoons) fresh chopped parsley
1 × 200-g (7-oz) can peeled tomatoes
salt and freshly-ground black pepper

Drain the chick peas and cook them in boiling water with the bicarbonate of soda for about 1½ hours. Drain them well.

Heat the oil in a flameproof casserole and fry the onion, garlic, celery and green pepper over a medium heat for 4–5 minutes, until the onion is transparent. Add the herbs, to-matoes and their juice and the chick peas. Season with salt and pepper and stir until the mixture bubbles. Cover the pan with a closely-fitting lid, or with foil, and cook in the preheated oven at 130°C (250°F), Gas ½, for at least 2½ hours.

In Greece, the pot is cooked all Saturday night long in a slow oven, and eaten for Sunday lunch.
Serves 4

WEST INDIAN BLACK-EYED BEANS

A spicy dish that can be served as a sauce with pasta or rice.

225 g (8 oz) dried black-eyed beans, soaked
60 ml (4 tablespoons) vegetable oil
1 large onion, peeled and chopped
1 clove garlic, peeled and crushed
5 ml (1 teaspoon) ground cinnamon
a large pinch of mixed spice
salt and freshly-ground black pepper
150 ml (¼ pint) chicken stock, or water and stock cube
30 ml (2 tablespoons) tomato purée
2 large tomatoes, skinned and quartered
15 ml (1 tablespoon) fresh chopped parsley

Drain the black-eyed beans and cook them in boiling water until they are tender – about 1½–2 hours. Drain them well.

Meanwhile, heat the oil in a pan and fry the onion and garlic over a medium heat for 4–5 minutes. Stir in the cinnamon, mixed spice, salt and pepper and continue to fry for a further 2 minutes. Add the beans, chicken stock, tomato purée and tomatoes, stir well and bring to the boil. Cover the pan and simmer for 15–20 minutes, until the sauce thickens. Check the seasoning and adjust if necessary. Pour over cooked rice or pasta and serve sprinkled with the parsley.
Serves 4

KITCHRI

45 ml (3 tablespoons) vegetable oil
1 large onion, peeled and chopped
1 clove garlic, peeled and crushed
5 ml (1 teaspoon) ground turmeric
5 ml (1 teaspoon) *garam masala*
a pinch of ground cloves
1 medium-sized potato, peeled and diced
2 large tomatoes, skinned and quartered
225 g (8 oz) dried mung beans, soaked
225 g (8 oz) brown rice
825 ml (1½ pints) water
salt
15 ml (1 tablespoon) lemon juice
15 g (½ oz) desiccated coconut

Heat the oil in a large pan and fry the onion and garlic over a medium heat for 4–5 minutes. Stir in the spices and cook for a further 2–3 minutes, stirring occasionally. Stir in the potato and tomatoes, then the drained beans and rice. Pour on the water, stir well and bring to the boil. Cover the pan and simmer until the beans and rice are tender – check after 50 minutes. Add the salt and lemon juice. If the dish is still runny, continue cooking in the uncovered pan until it is almost dry, stirring from time to time to prevent it from sticking. Garnish with the coconut before serving.

Serves 4

VEGETABLE KITCHRI

A highly nutritious dish, with layers of pulses, rice and vegetables, a colourful combination that is suitable for an informal
supper party.

225 g (8 oz) long-grain rice
salt
100 g (4 oz) brown lentils, washed
100 g (4 oz) red lentils, washed
60 ml (4 tablespoons) vegetable oil
1 large onion, peeled and sliced
2 cloves garlic, peeled and crushed
4-cm (1½-in) piece of fresh root ginger, peeled and finely
    chopped
5 ml (1 teaspoon) ground turmeric
2.5 ml (½ teaspoon) ground coriander
2.5 ml (½ teaspoon) paprika
2.5 ml (½ teaspoon) freshly-ground black pepper
1 large potato, peeled and diced
1 large carrot, peeled and thinly sliced
225 g (8 oz) French beans, trimmed and cut into 2.5-cm
    (1-in) pieces
1 small cauliflower, trimmed and cut into small florets
2 large tomatoes, skinned and quartered
15 ml (1 tablespoon) very finely chopped coriander leaves, if
    available (or use parsley)
450 ml (¾ pint) chicken stock, or water and stock cube, boiling

Partly cook the rice in boiling, salted water for 5 minutes, then
drain it into a colander and set aside. Partly cook the lentils
together in boiling water for 15 minutes, then drain them and
set them aside.

Meanwhile, prepare the vegetable mixture. Heat the oil in a
large pan and fry the onion, garlic and ginger over a medium
heat for 5–7 minutes, until the onion is just golden brown. Stir
in the spices, including the pepper, and cook for a further 2–3
minutes. Add the prepared vegetables, the coriander leaves and
2.5 ml (½ teaspoon) salt, cover the pan and simmer very gently
for 30 minutes, stirring occasionally.

Grease a large heatproof casserole and arrange layers of the vegetable mixture, lentils and rice in it. Pour on the boiling stock, cover the casserole and cook in the oven preheated to 150°C (300°F), Gas 2, for 1 hour, removing the lid for the last few minutes.

Serve very hot. Crusty French bread 'buttered' with garlic butter goes very well with this spicy dish.
Serves 6

VEGETABLE CURRY

Since so many people on the Indian Continent are forbidden to eat meat on religious grounds, many of the most authentic and delicious curry dishes are vegetarian.

45 ml (3 tablespoons) vegetable oil
1 large onion, peeled and sliced
2 cloves garlic, peeled and crushed
2.5-cm (1-in) piece root ginger, peeled and finely chopped
5 ml (1 teaspoon) ground turmeric
5 ml (1 teaspoon) paprika
5 ml (1 teaspoon) *garam masala*
2.5 ml (½ teaspoon) ground coriander
2.5 ml (½ teaspoon) ground cumin
2.5 ml (½ teaspoon) chilli powder
1.5 ml (¼ teaspoon) freshly-ground black pepper
450 g (1 lb) potatoes, peeled and diced
450 g (1 lb) young runner beans, trimmed and cut into 4-cm (1½-in) chunks
225 g (8 oz) broad beans (shelled weight)
100 g (4 oz) green peas (shelled weight)
30 ml (2 tablespoons) water
1 × 375-g (14-oz) can peeled tomatoes
30 ml (2 tablespoons) lemon juice
5 ml (1 teaspoon) salt
150 ml (¼ pint) natural yoghurt (optional)

Heat the oil in a large frying-pan and fry the onion, garlic and ginger over a medium heat for about 4–6 minutes, until the onion is just beginning to brown. Mix together the spices, including the pepper, and stir them into the pan. Reduce the heat and cook, stirring occasionally, for 3 minutes, for the spices to blend. Add the prepared vegetables and the water and cook, stirring from time to time, for 10 minutes. Add the tomatoes and their juice, lemon juice and salt, stir well, and bring to the boil. Cover the pan and simmer for 30 minutes. Stir in the yoghurt, if used, allow just to heat through, and serve hot.

You can accompany this curry, which is full of colour and different textures, with as many side dishes as you like – onion and pepper rings, diced cucumber stirred into natural yoghurt, slices of banana in lemon juice, desiccated coconut, fruit chutney and, of course, rice and poppadoms.
Serves 4–6

VEGETABLE DHAL

225 g (8 oz) red lentils, washed
600 ml (1 pint) water
2 medium-sized onions, peeled and chopped
5 ml (1 teaspoon) curry powder
salt
50 g (2 oz) butter, diced
30 ml (2 tablespoons) vegetable oil
1 clove garlic, peeled and crushed
10 ml (2 teaspoons) *garam masala*
2 large tomatoes, skinned and quartered
2 courgettes, trimmed and sliced
225 g (8 oz) broad beans, cooked (shelled weight)
225 g (8 oz) French beans, cooked and sliced

Put the lentils in a pan with the water, one of the onions and curry powder, bring to the boil and cook until the lentils are tender and have absorbed the water – about ¾–1 hour. Remove the pan from the heat, add salt and half the butter and beat with a wooden spoon until the mixture is smooth.

Meanwhile, heat the oil in a pan and fry the remaining onion and the garlic over a medium heat for 4–5 minutes. Stir in the *garam masala*, the tomatoes and courgettes and cook for 5 minutes, stirring occasionally. Stir in the broad beans and the

French beans, then carefully stir this vegetable mixture into the lentils. Reheat gently over a low heat. Taste and adjust seasoning if necessary, and stir in the remaining butter before serving.
Serves 4–6

CURRIED CHICK PEAS

325 g (12 oz) chick peas, soaked
a pinch of bicarbonate of soda
salt
45 ml (3 tablespoons) vegetable oil
1 large onion, peeled and sliced
2 cloves garlic, peeled and crushed
2.5-cm (1-in) piece fresh root ginger, peeled and finely chopped
1 large carrot, peeled and sliced
5 ml (1 teaspoon) cumin seeds
5 ml (1 teaspoon) ground coriander
5 ml (1 teaspoon) *garam masala*
2.5 ml ($\frac{1}{2}$ teaspoon) ground cumin
2.5 ml ($\frac{1}{2}$ teaspoon) ground turmeric
2.5 ml ($\frac{1}{2}$ teaspoon) chilli powder
2.5 ml ($\frac{1}{2}$ teaspoon) salt
150 ml ($\frac{1}{4}$ pint) chicken stock, or water and stock cube
100 g (4 oz) fresh green peas (shelled weight), or frozen ones, thawed
15 ml (1 tablespoon) fresh chopped parsley

Put the chick peas in a pan and cook in boiling water with the bicarbonate of soda, adding salt just before the peas are almost tender – about 2$\frac{1}{2}$ hours. Drain them well.

Meanwhile, heat the oil in a pan and fry the onion, garlic and ginger over a medium heat for 4–5 minutes, until the onion is transparent. Add the carrot and cumin seeds and stir-fry for 1 minute. Mix together the spices and stir them in with the salt. Fry for 2–3 minutes, stirring once or twice, then pour on the stock and bring to the boil. Add the cooked chick peas and the peas, stir and cover the pan. Simmer over a low heat for 45 minutes. Garnish with the parsley before serving.
Serves 6

SOYA CASSEROLE

A protein-packed dish to serve with fluffy rice and a fresh green vegetable.

  225 g (8 oz) dried soya beans, soaked
  a pinch of bicarbonate of soda
  2.5 ml (½ teaspoon) red pepper sauce
  1 bay leaf
  a few parsley stalks
  30 ml (2 tablespoons) vegetable oil
  1 large onion, peeled and sliced
  1 clove garlic, peeled and crushed
  2 stalks celery, thinly sliced
  2 large tomatoes, skinned and quartered
  30 ml (2 tablespoons) soya sauce
  45 ml (3 tablespoons) chicken stock, or dry white wine
  30 ml (2 tablespoons) fresh chopped parsley
  salt and freshly-ground black pepper

Drain the beans and cook them in boiling water with the bicarbonate of soda, red pepper sauce, and the bay leaf and parsley stalks tied together, until they are tender – about 3 hours. Remove the herbs and drain the beans well.

Heat the oil in a pan and fry the onion and garlic over a medium heat for 4–5 minutes, until the onion is transparent. Add the celery and fry, stirring once or twice, for another 5 minutes. Stir in the tomatoes, soya sauce, stock or wine and the beans, and bring to the boil. Cover the pan and simmer gently for 15 minutes. Stir in the parsley, season with salt and pepper and cook for 2–3 minutes more.

Serves 4

SOYA BEAN RISSOLES

  225 g (8 oz) dried soya beans, soaked
  a pinch of bicarbonate of soda
  2 stalks celery, halved
  15 ml (1 tablespoon) vegetable oil
  1 medium-sized onion, peeled and grated

5 ml (1 teaspoon) chilli powder
50 g (2 oz) cheese, grated
25 g (1 oz) walnuts, finely chopped
salt and freshly-ground black pepper
1 egg, lightly beaten
30 ml (2 tablespoons) fresh chopped parsley
fresh brown breadcrumbs
oil for frying
For the Yoghurt Sauce
1 clove garlic, peeled and crushed
2.5 ml ($\frac{1}{2}$ teaspoon) salt
300 ml ($\frac{1}{2}$ pint) natural yoghurt, chilled
15 ml (1 tablespoon) fresh chopped mint leaves
freshly-ground black pepper

Drain the beans and cook them in boiling water with the bicarbonate of soda and celery until they are tender – about 3
hours. Drain them well and discard the celery.

Heat the oil in a pan and fry the onion over a medium heat
for 4–5 minutes. Stir in the chilli powder, beans, cheese and
walnuts and season with salt and pepper. Stir well, remove the
pan from the heat and either put the mixture through a food
mill or liquidize in a blender. Beat in just enough of the egg to
give a firm, stiff dough, and stir in the parsley. Leave the mixture to chill in the refrigerator for 30 minutes.

Divide the mixture into eight and form it into sausage
shapes. Dip them in the breadcrumbs and fry in hot oil,
turning them so that they cook and brown evenly. Serve with
chilled yoghurt sauce.

To make the sauce, crush the garlic and mix it to a paste
with the salt. Stir it into the yoghurt with the mint, and
season with pepper. Serve well chilled.
Serves 4

FALAFEL

Chick pea balls are a national dish in Israel. You can make them with canned chick peas to save time.

450 g (1 lb) dried chick peas, soaked
a pinch of bicarbonate of soda
salt
1 large onion, peeled and sliced
1 clove garlic, peeled and crushed
50 g (2 oz) fresh brown breadcrumbs
15 ml (1 tablespoon) fresh chopped coriander leaves, if available (or use parsley)
15 ml (1 tablespoon) *tahina* (sesame seed paste), or olive oil
5 ml (1 teaspoon) salt
5 ml (1 teaspoon) ground coriander
2.5 ml ($\frac{1}{2}$ teaspoon) ground turmeric
2.5 ml ($\frac{1}{2}$ teaspoon) ground cumin
2.5 ml ($\frac{1}{2}$ teaspoon) freshly-ground black pepper
1.5 ml ($\frac{1}{4}$ teaspoon) chilli powder
juice of 1 lemon
1 egg, lightly beaten
40 g ($1\frac{1}{2}$ oz) flour
oil or fat for deep frying

Drain the chick peas and cook them in boiling water with the bicarbonate of soda, adding salt just before they are cooked – about 3 hours. Drain them well.

Mince the cooked chick peas with the onion and garlic twice, using the fine blade on the mincer. Mix the ground chick peas with the breadcrumbs, coriander, *tahina* or oil, spices and seasonings. Beat in the lemon juice and the egg to form a smooth paste. Add a little water if necessary. Cover and chill for 30 minutes.

Shape the mixture into 4-cm ($1\frac{1}{2}$-in) balls and roll them in the flour. Heat the oil or fat in a deep-frying pan until it reaches 180°C (350°F) on a thermometer, or a cube of bread dropped into the oil browns in about 45 seconds. Fry the chick pea balls a few at a time until they are golden. Remove them from the pan with a draining spoon and drain them on crumpled kitchen paper towels. Keep them warm while you fry the rest of the batch.

Serve the balls hot – they are usually accompanied by green salad.

Serves 4

CHICK PEA PATTIES

A less spicy way with ground chick peas.

225 g (8 oz) dried chick peas, soaked
a pinch of bicarbonate of soda
salt
225 g (8 oz) potatoes, peeled
salt
1 medium-sized onion, peeled and chopped
30 ml (2 tablespoons) fresh chopped parsley
freshly-ground black pepper
1 egg, lightly beaten
15 ml (1 tablespoon) lemon juice
40 g (1½ oz) flour
oil or fat for deep frying

Drain the chick peas and cook them in boiling water with the bicarbonate of soda, adding salt just before they are cooked – about 3 hours. Drain them well.

Meanwhile, cook the potatoes in boiling, salted water and drain them. Using the fine blade on the mincer, mince together the cooked chick peas, potatoes and onion, twice. Stir in the parsley and season the mixture with salt and pepper. Stir in the egg and lemon juice and beat with a wooden spoon. Cover the bowl and chill for 30 minutes – this makes the mixture easier to handle.

Shape the mixture into small flat cakes and roll them in the flour. Heat the oil or fat until it reaches 180°C (350°F) on a thermometer or a cube of bread dropped into the oil browns in about 45 seconds. Fry patties until they are golden brown. Remove them from the pan and drain them on crumpled kitchen paper towels.

Serve the patties with green salad.

Serves 4

LENTIL RISSOLES

You can prepare the rissoles in advance and leave them in the
refrigerator, ready to cook.

225 g (8 oz) red lentils, washed
300 ml (½ pint) water
30 ml (2 tablespoons) vegetable oil
1 medium-sized onion, peeled and chopped
salt and freshly-ground black pepper
2.5 ml (½ teaspoon) ground coriander
2.5 ml (½ teaspoon) ground cumin
a large pinch of chilli powder
15 ml (1 tablespoon) lemon juice
1 egg, beaten
25 g (1 oz) flour
oil or fat for frying

Put the lentils in a pan with the water. Bring to the boil, cover
the pan and simmer until the lentils are soft and have absorbed
the water – about ¾–1 hour. Check during this time and add a
little more boiling water if necessary, to prevent the lentils from
sticking. If the lentils are soft but still wet, cook for about 2
minutes in the uncovered pan until the moisture is driven off.
Liquidize them in a blender or put them through a food mill.

Heat the oil in a pan and fry the onion over a medium heat
until it is transparent, then stir in the spices and seasonings.
Cook for 4–5 minutes. Beat in the lentil purée, lemon juice and
enough of the egg to form a firm, stiff dough. Cover the dough
and chill it for about 30 minutes, to make it easier to handle.

Shape into flat, round cakes and dust them lightly with flour.
Fry them in hot oil for about 5 minutes on each side, until they
are evenly browned. Drain them on crumpled kitchen paper
towels.

Serve the rissoles hot, either with green salad, or with
tomato sauce and a green vegetable.

Serves 4

LENTIL ROLL

Almost a classic in vegetarian cooking, a tasty, spicy roast.

325 g (12 oz) red lentils, washed
about 450 ml (¾ pint) water
50 g (2 oz) butter
1 large onion, peeled and chopped
15 ml (1 tablespoon) fresh chopped mint, or 2.5 ml (½ teaspoon) mixed dried herbs
15 ml (1 tablespoon) lemon juice
1 egg, lightly beaten
salt and freshly-ground black pepper
5 ml (1 teaspoon) ground coriander
about 25 g (1 oz) fresh brown breadcrumbs
25 g (1 oz) flour
60 ml (4 tablespoons) vegetable oil

Put the lentils in a pan with just enough water to cover. Bring to the boil, cover the pan and simmer until the lentils have absorbed the water and are soft – about ¾–1 hour. Stir occasionally during this time and add a little more water if necessary. Dry the lentils off in the uncovered pan if they are cooked but still runny.

Melt the butter in a pan and fry the onion over a medium heat until it is transparent. Beat the onion, mint, lemon juice and egg into the lentils, season with the salt, pepper and coriander, and add enough breadcrumbs to form a firm paste. Turn the mixture on to a lightly-floured board and shape it into a roll. Dust it lightly with flour.

Pour the oil into a small baking dish. Carefully lift the roll into the dish and bake in the oven preheated to 190°C (375°F), Gas 5, for 50–60 minutes, until the roll is crisp. Cover it with foil towards the end of the cooking time if it is browning too much. Lift it on to kitchen paper towels to absorb any traces of oil. Serve hot.

You can serve this lentil roll with a meat dish – it is especially good with baked or boiled bacon or ham – or as a vegetarian main dish with tomato sauce and green salad tossed with cubes of cheese.

Serves 4–6

VEGETABLE PAELLA

Full of colour and interest, yet surprisingly inexpensive to make.

75 ml (5 tablespoons) vegetable oil
2 large onions, peeled and chopped
2 cloves garlic, peeled and crushed
1 red and 1 green pepper, trimmed and thinly sliced
2 stalks celery, thinly sliced
325 g (12 oz) long-grain rice
600 ml (1 pint) chicken stock, or water and stock cube
3 large tomatoes, skinned and quartered
225 g (8 oz) French beans, trimmed and cut into 5-cm (2-in) pieces
100 g (4 oz) fresh green peas (shelled weight)
salt and freshly-ground black pepper
12 stuffed olives, sliced
15 ml (1 tablespoon) fresh chopped marjoram (or use parsley)

In a large pan, heat the oil and fry the onions, garlic, red and green pepper and celery over a medium heat for 5–6 minutes, stirring occasionally. Stir in the rice and cook, stirring occasionally, for a further 5 minutes. Pour on the stock and add the tomatoes. Bring the stock to the boil, add the beans and peas and season well with salt and pepper. Return the liquid to the boil, stir well, cover the pan and simmer over a low heat for 30 minutes, without stirring. Check that the rice is tender. Add a little boiling water and cook for a further 5–10 minutes if necessary. Stir in the sliced olives. Garnish with the marjoram before serving.
Serves 4–6

OMELETTE CLAMART

Soft, subtly flavoured pea purée makes a delightful filling for this classic omelette.

4 large eggs
salt and freshly-ground black pepper

15 ml (1 tablespoon) cold water
5 ml (1 teaspoon) fresh chopped chives
15 g (½ oz) unsalted butter
30 ml (2 tablespoons) pea purée (see page 82)
5 ml (1 teaspoon) double cream

Break the eggs into a bowl, whisk lightly with a fork and season with salt and pepper. Add the cold water and whisk again with a fork. Stir in the chopped chives.

Melt the butter in a small, heavy-based frying-pan or omelette pan and place over a high heat until the butter is foaming. Do not let it brown. Pour in the eggs and stir with the fork. As the omelette begins to set, lift the edge all round with a fish slice or palette knife. When the bottom of the omelette has set but the top is still running, shake the pan briskly a few times. Mix the pea purée and cream together and spread over one half of the omelette. Tilt the pan and fold the omelette in half, using a fish slice or palette knife. Slide the omelette on to a heated plate or serving dish. Cut it in half and serve at once.
Serves 2

SPRING OMELETTES

These are filled with one or more cold, cooked vegetables – a perfect and economical way to use left-overs. Large vegetables must be shredded or finely chopped. Try cold, cooked French beans chopped small and stirred with a finely-chopped spring onion and double cream. Or very small cooked (or canned) broad beans, 2.5 ml (½ teaspoon) dried basil and double cream. Or cooked (or canned) and drained dried white haricot beans stirred into melted butter with a crushed garlic clove and 5 ml (1 teaspoon) fresh chopped parsley.

PICNIC OMELETTES

These omelettes, little envelopes enclosing a light, creamy filling, are eaten cold. Use a very small frying-pan to make wafer-thin omelettes that are light and crisp. Serve two for each portion.

45 ml (3 tablespoons) cream cheese
45 ml (3 tablespoons) single cream
salt
a pinch of cayenne pepper
1 spring onion, trimmed and thinly sliced
1 × 175-g (6-oz) can flageolets, drained
40 g (1½ oz) unsalted butter
8 large eggs
30 ml (2 tablespoons) cold water

Mix together the cream cheese and single cream and beat well.
Season with salt and cayenne pepper and stir in the spring
onion and flageolets.

Melt the butter in a very small frying-pan, about 12 cm (5 in)
in diameter, over a high heat. Mix the eggs in a bowl with a
fork and stir in the water. When the butter starts to foam,
measure 45 ml (3 tablespoons) of the egg mixture into the pan.
Stir with a fork and cook until the underside has set and the
top is still runny. Spoon a little filling on to one side of the
omelette, flip it in half and slide it on to a plate. Repeat until all
the egg and filling mixtures are used.

Serve cold, garnished with fresh chopped herbs.

Serves 4

SPANISH OMELETTE

You can make these as individual as you wish, by including
whatever vegetables you have on hand. A good balance of
different shapes, colours and textures is important.

45 ml (3 tablespoons) olive oil
1 medium-sized potato, peeled and diced
1 large onion, peeled and sliced
1 small red pepper, trimmed and chopped
salt
75 g (3 oz) baby broad beans, cooked (shelled weight)
4 eggs
freshly-ground black pepper

Heat the oil in a frying-pan and fry the potato, onion and red pepper over a medium heat for 2 minutes, stirring. Season with salt, cover the pan and cook over a low heat for 15 minutes. Stir in the beans and heat through.

Beat the eggs lightly. Transfer the vegetable mixture to the bowl with the eggs, using a draining spoon, and season with pepper. Mix with a fork. Pour off most of the oil in the pan. Reheat the remaining oil, then pour in the egg mixture. Stir with a fork and, as the eggs begin to set, shake the pan to prevent the omelette from sticking. When the underside is lightly cooked, put the pan under a hot grill momentarily, to set the top. Slide the omelette on to a heated serving dish or plate, to eat hot. Cut into wedges. Alternatively, the omelette may be served cold, with salad, or as a cold filling in hot, split pitta bread.

Serves 4

AMERICAN POP-OVERS

100 g (4 oz) wholemeal flour
a pinch of salt
2 eggs
150 ml ($\frac{1}{4}$ pint) milk
30 ml (2 tablespoons) water

For the Filling
25 g (1 oz) butter
1 small onion, peeled and grated
1 stalk celery, finely chopped
2 large tomatoes, skinned and quartered
1 red pepper, trimmed and chopped
2.5 ml ($\frac{1}{2}$ teaspoon) chilli powder
175 g (6 oz) dried haricot beans, cooked
15 ml (1 tablespoon) fresh chopped parsley

Brush 12 deep patty tins with a little vegetable oil. Put the flour and salt into a bowl, make a well in the centre and break in the eggs. Beat well, then gradually add the milk and water, beating all the time. Heat the patty tins, then pour in the batter and bake in the oven preheated to 220°C (425°F), Gas 7, for 15–20 minutes, until the pop-overs are well risen and golden brown.

Meanwhile, melt the butter in a small pan and cook the onion, celery, tomatoes and red pepper to a smooth paste, beating from time to time with a wooden spoon. Add the chilli powder, beans and parsley, season with salt and heat through.

When they are cooked, transfer the pop-overs to a heated serving dish and spoon the hot sauce over them. Serve at once.
Serves 6

PITTA BREAD WITH HOT BEAN SAUCE

A very informal way with beans – a hot, spicy sauce used as a filling for pitta – a kind of bean sandwich.

60 ml (4 tablespoons) olive oil
325 g (12 oz) tomatoes, skinned and chopped
1 × 100-g (4-oz) can pimentos, chopped (reserve the liquor from the can)
2 cloves garlic, peeled and crushed
1 × 75-g (3-oz) can tomato purée
salt and freshly-ground black pepper
2.5 ml (½ teaspoon) cayenne pepper
2.5 ml (½ teaspoon) dried oregano
2.5 ml (½ teaspoon) sugar
225 g (8 oz) dried black beans, cooked
15 ml (1 tablespoon) red wine vinegar
pitta bread to serve, hot

Heat the oil in a pan and add the tomatoes. Mash them with a wooden spoon and cook over a medium heat for about 5 minutes. Add the chopped pimentos, 30 ml (2 tablespoons) of liquor from the can, the garlic and tomato purée and season with salt, pepper, cayenne pepper, oregano and sugar. Cover the pan and cook the sauce until it has thickened (about 20–25 minutes). Stir in the beans and vinegar and cook, uncovered, for 5 minutes more. Split pieces of hot pitta bread and stuff them with the spiced beans. Provide plenty of paper napkins to serve.
Serves 4

CANNELLONI WITH BEANS

An adaptation of a popular pasta dish.

16 small tubes of cannelloni ('instant' type if available)
30 ml (2 tablespoons) olive oil
1 large onion, peeled and finely chopped
2 cloves garlic, peeled and crushed
1 × 200-g (7-oz) can peeled tomatoes
30 ml (2 tablespoons) tomato purée
2.5 ml (½ teaspoon) sugar
5 ml (1 teaspoon) dried oregano
5 ml (1 teaspoon) white wine vinegar
salt and freshly-ground black pepper
175 g (6 oz) dried borlotti beans, cooked
25 g (1 oz) butter
25 g (1 oz) flour
450 ml (¾ pint) milk
a pinch of nutmeg
25 g (1 oz) Parmesan cheese, grated

If the cannelloni is not the instant type, cook it in boiling, salted water as directed on the packet, drain it and set it aside.

Heat the oil in a pan and fry the onion and garlic over a medium heat until the onion is transparent. Add the tomatoes and their juice, the tomato purée, sugar, oregano, vinegar, salt and pepper. Stir well and cover the pan. Simmer very gently for 45 minutes, checking from time to time that the mixture has not dried out. Add a very little water if necessary. Spread a little of the tomato mixture over the base of a shallow oven-proof dish. Stir the beans into the remaining filling and fill the cannelloni tubes. Arrange the cannelloni in the dish and pour over any remaining filling.

While the filling is cooking, make a white sauce with the butter, flour and milk, season with salt, pepper and nutmeg and stir in the cheese. Pour the sauce over the cannelloni. Cover the dish with foil and bake in the oven preheated to 180°C (350°F), Gas 4, for 30–35 minutes, removing the foil for the last few minutes to brown the sauce.

Serves 4

CHINESE SPRING ROLLS

Whether they are served as an accompaniment to a full Chinese meal, or simply with rice pilaf, these crispy little pancakes are always popular.

325 g (12 oz) flour
225 ml (8 fl. oz) water
1 egg, lightly beaten
45 ml (3 tablespoons) vegetable oil
5 ml (1 teaspoon) salt
225 g (8 oz) fresh bean sprouts (or canned ones, drained and rinsed)
225 g (8 oz) mushrooms, wiped and thinly sliced
6 spring onions, trimmed and thinly sliced
30 ml (2 tablespoons) soya sauce
1.5 ml ($\frac{1}{4}$ teaspoon) freshly-ground black pepper
oil for deep frying

To make the pastry, put the flour in a bowl, gradually pour on the water and half the beaten egg, and mix to a smooth paste. Knead until it is smooth. On a lightly-floured board, roll into a large, thin sheet. Divide the paste into 12 equal pieces, about 15 cm (6 in) square.

Heat the oil in a heavy frying-pan and add the salt, bean sprouts, mushrooms and spring onions. Stir-fry over a high heat for 1 minute, reduce the heat to medium and stir-fry for a further minute. Pour on the soya sauce, season with pepper and stir to coat the vegetables in the sauce. Remove the pan from the heat and allow the filling to cool.

Divide the cooled filling between the 12 paste squares. To roll each pancake, fold in two parallel sides and then roll Swiss-roll fashion, with the tucked-in edges at the sides. Moisten the edges with beaten egg and pinch them firmly to seal.

Heat the oil in a deep-frying pan until it reaches 180°C (350°F) on a thermometer, or a cube of bread dropped into the oil browns in about 45 seconds. Fry the spring rolls in batches for 3–4 minutes. until they are crisp and golden brown. Remove the cooked rolls from the pan with a draining spoon

and drain on crumpled kitchen paper towels. Keep them warm in a hot towel while you cook the remaining rolls. Serve hot.
Makes 12

BROAD BEANS AU GRATIN

1 kg (2¼ lb) fresh broad beans (shelled weight)
salt
50 g (2 oz) butter
225 g (8 oz) button mushrooms, wiped and trimmed
25 g (1 oz) flour
300 ml (½ pint) milk
freshly-ground black pepper
15 ml (1 tablespoon) fresh very finely chopped chives
30 ml (2 tablespoons) fresh soured cream
15 g (½ oz) Parmesan cheese, grated

Cook the beans in boiling, salted water until they are just tender – about 10–12 minutes. Drain them well.

Melt half the butter in a pan and fry the mushrooms over a gentle heat for 3–4 minutes. Set aside. Melt the remaining butter in a second small pan, stir in the flour and cook until it forms a ball. Gradually pour on the milk, stirring, and bring to the boil. Add salt and pepper and the chives and simmer, stirring, for 3 minutes. Stir in the soured cream, beans and mushrooms. Turn the vegetables into a flameproof dish, sprinkle the cheese over and brown under the grill. A crisp green salad is a good accompaniment.
Serves 4

STUFFED COURGETTES

You can use this, and the other fillings in this section, to fill aubergines, peppers, large onions or marrows, or enclose it in cabbage or vine leaves.

50 g (2 oz) butter
15 ml (1 tablespoon) olive oil
1 medium-sized onion, peeled and finely chopped
2 cloves garlic, peeled and crushed
4 large tomatoes, skinned and chopped
salt and freshly-ground black pepper
15 ml (1 tablespoon) fresh chopped mint leaves
5 ml (1 teaspoon) fresh chopped parsley
100 g (4 oz) dried white haricot beans, cooked (or canned ones, drained)
4 large courgettes
25 g (1 oz) Parmesan cheese, grated
15 g (½ oz) fresh white breadcrumbs

Heat half the butter and all of the oil in a pan and fry the onion and garlic over a medium heat until they are transparent. Add the tomatoes, salt, pepper and herbs and continue cooking, stirring occasionally, for about 5 minutes. Stir in the beans, and remove the pan from the heat.

Meanwhile, blanch the courgettes in boiling, salted water for about 2 minutes. Cut them in half lengthways, scoop out and discard the seeds. Arrange the courgette halves in a shallow, buttered ovenproof dish. Divide the filling between them, piling it up and smoothing it into a neat mound. Melt the remaining butter. Combine the cheese and the breadcrumbs and spoon them over the vegetables, particularly over the filling. Pour the melted butter over, and bake in the oven preheated to 180°C (350°F), Gas 4, for 20–25 minutes, until the topping is crisp and golden brown.

Serves 4

BAKED ONION CUPS

Choose large onions of an even size and fill them brim full of colourful vegetables.

4 large Spanish onions, peeled
salt
30 ml (2 tablespoons) vegetable oil
1 green pepper, trimmed and chopped
2 large tomatoes, skinned and chopped
2.5 ml ($\frac{1}{2}$ teaspoon) dried sage
50 g (2 oz) long-grain rice, cooked
50 g (2 oz) dried aduki beans, cooked
freshly-ground black pepper
50 g (2 oz) Parmesan cheese, grated
50 g (2 oz) ground almonds
150 ml ($\frac{1}{4}$ pint) natural yoghurt
1 egg white, stiffly beaten

Blanch the onions in boiling, salted water for 5 minutes, drain them in a colander and refresh them under cold running water. Drain them and pat them dry. Cut the top from each onion and scoop out enough of the centre to leave a firm 'wall' all round. Chop the scooped-out flesh and set aside the onion cups.

Heat the oil in a pan and fry the green pepper over a medium heat for 2–3 minutes. Add the chopped onion, tomatoes and sage and cook for a further 2 minutes. Stir in the rice and beans, and season the mixture with salt and pepper. Fill the onion cups with the stuffing, piling it up and shaping it into a mound. Arrange the onions in a well-greased ovenproof casserole just large enough to hold them upright, in one layer.

Beat the cheese and ground almonds into the yoghurt and fold in the egg white. Spoon over the onions and bake in the oven preheated to 180°C (350°F), Gas 4, for 50 minutes–1 hour, until the onions are soft and the topping is well risen and golden brown.

Serves 4

MARROW WITH CHEESE STUFFING

This is a Greek way of serving marrow, an inspired combination of vegetables and herbs.

  1 medium-sized vegetable marrow
  30 ml (2 tablespoons) olive oil
  1 large onion, peeled and grated
  450 ml (¾ pint) water, boiling
  100 g (4 oz) long-grain rice
  45 ml (3 tablespoons) fresh chopped mint leaves
  salt and freshly-ground black pepper
  75 g (3 oz) dried white haricot beans, cooked
  50 g (2 oz) feta (or use Wensleydale) cheese, diced
  8 outside leaves of lettuce
  a few mint sprigs

Cut a small slice from each end of the marrow and reserve. Using a teaspoon or vegetable baller, and working from each end in turn, scoop out and discard all the seeds.

Put the olive oil, onion and boiling water into a pan, bring to the boil and simmer for 10 minutes. Add the rice and mint, season with salt and pepper, stir well and cover the pan. Simmer without stirring for about 20–25 minutes, until the rice is cooked and has absorbed the water. Remove the pan from the heat and stir in the beans and the cheese.

Pack the filling into the marrow and shape the two end slices so that they fit into the openings like plugs. Arrange 4 lettuce leaves in an ovenproof dish. Place the stuffed marrow on the leaves. Wrap any left-over filling in a piece of foil, shape into a roll and place beside the marrow. Cover the marrow with the remaining lettuce leaves. Pour on about 600 ml (1 pint) of boiling water, cover the dish with a lid or foil and bake in the oven preheated to 180°C (350°F), Gas 4, for 40–45 minutes. Discard the lettuce leaves. Remove the filling from the foil, cut it into slices and arrange in an overlapping line along the top of the marrow. Garnish with mint sprigs before serving.
Serves 6

STUFFED CABBAGE LEAVES

An attractive way to present a small portion of cooked, dried beans.

  8 tender young cabbage leaves
  salt
  75 g (3 oz) butter
  2 medium-sized onions, peeled and chopped
  1 clove garlic, peeled and crushed
  450 g (1 lb) tomatoes, skinned
  75 g (3 oz) dried aduki beans, cooked (or other cooked dried
    beans)
  25 g (1 oz) pine nuts
  15 ml (1 tablespoon) fresh chopped parsley
  freshly-ground black pepper
  25 g (1 oz) Parmesan cheese, grated

Trim the cabbage leaves and blanch them in boiling, salted water for 4–5 minutes, until they are soft enough to roll. Drain them and refresh them in cold running water, then pat them dry.

Melt half the butter in a pan and fry the onion and garlic over a medium heat until they are transparent. Remove the pan from the heat. Add three-quarters of the tomatoes, the beans, pine nuts and parsley, and season with salt and pepper. Stir the mixture well and simmer until it forms a thick pulp.

Spread the cabbage leaves flat on a board and divide the filling between them. Roll up each leaf to enclose the filling completely and tie it with twine.

Melt the remaining butter in an ovenproof casserole and arrange the cabbage parcels in it. Slice the remaining tomatoes and arrange them on top. Baste with the butter, cover and bake in the oven preheated to 180°C (350°F), Gas 4, for 45–50 minutes. Sprinkle the cheese on top and return the uncovered casserole to the oven until it melts.

Serves 4

STUFFED AUBERGINES

    4 medium-sized aubergines
    salt
    50 g (2 oz) butter
    2 medium-sized onions, peeled and chopped
    3 large tomatoes, skinned and quartered
    75 g (3 oz) dried gungo peas, cooked (or other cooked, dried
        beans)
    freshly-ground black pepper
    75 g (3 oz) cheese, grated
    25 g (1 oz) fresh brown breadcrumbs

Trim the stalks from the aubergines, wash them and cut them in half lengthways. Sprinkle the cut sides with salt and leave them in a colander over a plate to drain for about 30 minutes. Wash the aubergines and dry them. Using a teaspoon or vegetable baller, scoop the seeds from the aubergines, leaving a 'channel' for the filling. Reserve the seeds.

Melt the butter in a pan and fry the onion over a medium heat until it is transparent. Add the reserved seeds and tomatoes and cook, stirring, for 2–3 minutes. Add the peas and season with salt and pepper. Remove from the heat.

Arrange the aubergines, cut side up, in one layer in a well-greased ovenproof dish and spoon the filling over them, patting it down well. Combine the cheese and breadcrumbs and sprinkle over the top. Pour on any fat left in the pan. Cover the dish with foil and bake in the oven preheated to 180°C (350°F), Gas 4, for 30 minutes. Remove the foil and return the dish to the oven for a further 5–10 minutes to brown the topping.
Serves 4

STUFFED GREEN PEPPERS

    4 large green peppers
    50 g (2 oz) butter
    2 small onions, peeled and finely chopped
    1 clove garlic, peeled and crushed

175 g (6 oz) cooked dried haricot beans (or canned ones, drained)

1 × 200-g (7-oz) can peeled tomatoes

2.5 ml ($\frac{1}{2}$ teaspoon) dried thyme

salt and freshly-ground black pepper

15 ml (1 tablespoon) lemon juice

5 ml (1 teaspoon) tomato purée

150 ml ($\frac{1}{4}$ pint) chicken stock, or water and stock cube

50 g (2 oz) cheese, grated

Cut the stalks from the peppers, cut a slice from the top of each and scoop out the white pith and seeds.

Melt the butter in a pan and fry half the onions and the garlic over a medium heat for 4–5 minutes. Add the cooked beans, one of the tomatoes and the thyme, and season with salt and pepper. Stir well and cook gently for 3–4 minutes.

Stand the peppers in an ovenproof dish just large enough to hold them upright, and fill them with this mixture.

Fry the remaining onion in the pan, stir in the rest of the tomatoes and their juice, the lemon juice and tomato purée, and season well. Pour on the stock, stir and bring slowly to the boil. Cover the pan and simmer for 10 minutes. Liquidize the sauce in a blender, or rub it through a sieve, and pour it over the peppers. Cover with a lid or foil and bake in the oven pre-heated to 180°C (350°F), Gas 4, for 1 hour. Sprinkle on the cheese and return the dish, uncovered, to the oven until it bubbles, or put it under a hot grill.

Serves 4

RATATOUILLE

You can serve this mixed vegetable dish hot with rice and French bread, or cold as a starter.

60 ml (4 tablespoons) olive oil
2 medium-sized onions, peeled and sliced
2 large cloves garlic, peeled and crushed
4 large tomatoes, skinned and chopped
1 green pepper, trimmed and sliced
450 g (1 lb) courgettes, trimmed and sliced
1 small aubergine, trimmed, sliced and dégorged
salt and freshly-ground black pepper
175 g (6 oz) cooked dried haricot beans (or canned ones, drained)
15 ml (1 tablespoon) fresh chopped parsley

Heat the oil in a pan and fry the onions and garlic over a medium heat until they are transparent. Add the tomatoes, green pepper, courgettes and aubergine and season well with salt and pepper. Cover the pan and cook for 30 minutes, stirring occasionally. Add the beans and parsley, cover the pan and simmer for a further 10 minutes. If the ratatouille is runny, remove the lid and slightly increase the heat to thicken the liquid.
Serves 4

AUBERGINE MOULD

An impressive way to serve a colourful mixture of vegetables. Prepare in advance, by having some cooked rice and beans ready.

90 ml (6 tablespoons) olive oil
675 g (1½ lb) aubergines, trimmed, thinly sliced and dégorged
1 kg (2¼ lb) tomatoes, skinned and chopped
2 cloves garlic, peeled and crushed
salt and freshly-ground black pepper
100 g (4 oz) long-grain rice, cooked
175 g (6 oz) dried mung beans, cooked
175 g (6 oz) cheese, grated

15 ml (1 tablespoon) fresh chopped parsley
3 eggs, lightly beaten

Butter a 20-cm (8-in) loose-bottomed cake tin or mould and put it on baking sheet.

Heat the oil in a frying-pan and fry the aubergine slices, a few at a time, until they just begin to change colour. Remove them with a draining spoon and drain on kitchen paper towels. Add more oil to the pan if necessary. In the same pan, fry the tomatoes and garlic well seasoned with salt and pepper. Stir often and cook until the tomatoes form a thick paste. Add the rice, beans, cheese and parsley, mix well, and remove the pan from the heat. Cool slightly, then stir in the beaten eggs. Beat gently with a wooden spoon.

Line the buttered tin or mould with overlapping slices of aubergine, making sure there are no gaps. Fill the mould with the tomato mixture and cover with more aubergine slices. Cover with buttered foil and bake in the oven preheated to 190°C (375°F), Gas 5, for 35–40 minutes. Allow to cool slightly in the tin, so that the aubergines shrink a little from the sides. Remove the foil and invert a heated serving dish over the mould. Turn it over and shake to release the vegetable 'cake'.
Serves 6

BEAN MOUSSAKA

An adaptation of the popular Greek dish.

675 g (1½ lb) aubergines
salt
90 ml (6 tablespoons) vegetable oil
2 large onions, peeled and sliced
1 clove garlic, peeled and crushed
450 g (1 lb) tomatoes, skinned and sliced
225 g (8 oz) dried butter beans, cooked (or use canned ones, drained)
salt and freshly-ground black pepper
25 g (1 oz) flour
3 eggs
300 ml (½ pint) natural yoghurt
75 g (3 oz) cheese, grated

Cut the stalks from the aubergines, wash them and slice them diagonally. Sprinkle the slices with salt and put them in a colander over a plate to drain for about 30 minutes. Wash the slices and dry them.

Heat the oil in a frying-pan and fry the aubergine slices a few at a time, turning them once. Remove them with a draining spoon and drain on kitchen paper towels while you fry the remaining slices. Do not let them brown. Add more oil if necessary. In the same pan, fry the onions and garlic over a medium heat until they are lightly browned. Add the tomatoes and cook for a further 5 minutes.

In a shallow ovenproof dish, arrange a layer of aubergine slices, sprinkle with some of the tomato mixture and half the beans. Season well with salt and pepper and continue with these layers, finishing with aubergines.

Beat the flour, eggs, yoghurt and cheese together, season with salt and pepper and pour over the aubergines. Bake in the oven preheated to 200°C (400°F), Gas 6, for 40–45 minutes, until the topping is golden brown.

Serve with green salad.

Serves 4

GREEK PASTITIO

A perfect dish for an informal buffet supper party. It is one of those vegetable dishes that looks and tastes as if it is full of meat.

175 g (6 oz) brown lentils, washed
450 ml ($\frac{3}{4}$ pint) water
60 ml (4 tablespoons) olive oil
40 g ($1\frac{1}{2}$ oz) butter
2 medium-sized onions, peeled and finely chopped
2 medium-sized aubergines, trimmed, cubed and dégorged
1 clove garlic, peeled and crushed
1 × 675-g ($1\frac{1}{2}$-lb) can peeled tomatoes
60 ml (4 tablespoons) tomato purée
5 ml (1 teaspoon) dried oregano
salt and freshly-ground black pepper
2.5 ml ($\frac{1}{2}$ teaspoon) sugar

450 g (1 lb) green ribbon noodles
25 g (1 oz) Parmesan cheese, grated

For the Sauce
40 g (1½ oz) butter
40 g (1½ oz) flour
600 ml (1 pint) milk
150 ml (¼ pint) natural yoghurt
3 eggs, lightly beaten
a large pinch of nutmeg
25 g (1 oz) Parmesan cheese, grated

Cook the lentils in the water until they are just tender but not mushy – about ¾–1 hour.

While they are cooking, heat the oil and butter in a large pan and fry the onions over a medium heat for 3–4 minutes. Add the aubergines to the pan with the garlic, cover and sweat the vegetables over a low heat for 15 minutes. Stir in the tomatoes and their juice, tomato purée, oregano, salt, pepper and sugar. Cover the pan and simmer for a further 10–15 minutes, until the tomatoes form a thick paste, then remove the pan from the heat.

Cook the noodles in boiling, salted water according to the directions on the packet, until they are just tender. Drain them in a colander and refresh them in cold water. Drain them well.

Butter a large, deep ovenproof dish and spread half the noodles over the base. Season with salt and pepper, sprinkle a little grated cheese over them, then spread the lentils and half the tomato sauce on top. Repeat the layers of noodles, seasoning, cheese, lentils and tomato sauce and level off the top.

To make the sauce, melt the butter in a small pan, stir in the flour and cook until it forms a ball. Gradually pour on the milk, stirring, and bring to the boil. Reduce the heat, stir in the yoghurt and season with salt, pepper and nutmeg. Cook the sauce, stirring, for 3 minutes. Stir in the cheese and pour the sauce over the pie.

Stand the dish on a baking sheet in case it bubbles over and bake in the oven preheated to 200°C (400°F), Gas 6, for 50 minutes–1 hour, until it is crispy brown on the outside.
Serves 8

LENTILS AND NOODLES IN TOMATO SAUCE

A Greek country recipe, which is often served during Lent and on other fast days.

    225 g (8 oz) green noodles
    salt
    225 g (8 oz) brown lentils, washed
    30 ml (2 tablespoons) tomato purée
    600 ml (1 pint) water
    1 medium-sized onion, peeled and chopped
    1 clove garlic, peeled and crushed
    5 ml (1 teaspoon) dried oregano
    60 ml (4 tablespoons) olive oil
    freshly-ground black pepper
    15 ml (1 tablespoon) fresh chopped parsley
    grated cheese to serve

Cook the noodles in boiling, salted water until they are just tender – follow the directions on the packet for the exact time, and drain them.

Meanwhile, put the lentils into a pan. Stir the tomato purée into the water and pour it over the lentils. Add the onion, garlic, oregano and olive oil and season with salt and pepper. Stir well. Bring to the boil, cover the pan and simmer until the lentils are tender – $\frac{3}{4}$–1 hour. Check from time to time and add a little more boiling water if necessary. Stir in the cooked noodles, check seasoning and add more if needed. Garnish with the parsley before serving and serve the grated cheese separately.
Serves 4

AUBERGINE AND BEAN SANDWICH

    1 kg (2¼ lb) potatoes, peeled
    salt
    30 ml (2 tablespoons) vegetable oil
    2 large onions, peeled and sliced
    450 g (1 lb) aubergines, trimmed, sliced and dégorged

225 g (8 oz) dried chick peas, cooked (or canned ones,
  drained)
freshly-ground black pepper
225 g (8 oz) cheese, grated
1 egg, beaten
150 ml (¼ pint) natural yoghurt

Partly cook the potatoes in boiling, salted water for 10 minutes,
then drain and slice them.

Heat the oil in a pan and fry the onions over a medium heat
until they are transparent. Arrange the vegetables in layers in a
greased ovenproof dish, seasoning between each layer and
sprinkling with cheese. Mix the remaining cheese and the egg
into the yoghurt, season with salt and pepper and pour over
the dish. Bake in the oven preheated to 190°C (375°F), Gas 5,
for about 1¼–1½ hours, until the vegetables are very soft and
the topping is golden brown.
Serves 6

BEAN AND MUSHROOM FLAN

Wholemeal pastry is not just to tempt us in the health food
restaurants – it's a marvellous base for imaginative mixtures of
vegetables.

175 g (6 oz) stone-ground wholemeal plain flour
1.5 ml (¼ teaspoon) salt
100 g (4 oz) margarine
cold water to mix
25 g (1 oz) butter
100 g (4 oz) mushrooms, wiped and sliced
1 × 100-g (4-oz) carton cottage cheese with chives
2 eggs
150 ml (¼ pint) milk
salt and freshly-ground black pepper
100 g (4 oz) broad beans, cooked (shelled weight)

Put the flour and salt in a bowl, cut in the margarine and rub it
in until the mixture resembles fine breadcrumbs. Add a very
little water – about 15 ml (1 tablespoon) to make a firm dough.
Turn on to a lightly-floured board, knead lightly to make a

smooth paste and roll out. Use to line a greased 12-cm (8½-in)
flan ring on a greased baking sheet. Trim the edges and prick
the base with a fork.

Melt the butter in a small pan and lightly fry the mushrooms
for 2–3 minutes over a low heat. Allow them to cool.

Beat together the cottage cheese, eggs and milk and season
with salt and pepper. Stir in the beans and mushrooms and
mix well. Pour into the prepared flan case. Bake in the oven
preheated to 180°C (350°F), Gas 4, for 35–40 minutes, until
the pastry is crisp and the filling set. Allow to cool in the flan
ring before transferring to a serving plate.
Serves 6

BUTTER BEAN FLAN

Cooked or canned butter beans make an unusual savoury flan
filling.

    225 g (8 oz) shortcrust pastry
    225 g (8 oz) dried butter beans, cooked (or canned ones,
       drained)
    2 eggs
    150 ml (¼ pint) milk
    150 ml (¼ pint) natural yoghurt
    salt and freshly-ground black pepper
    5 ml (1 teaspoon) fresh chopped chives
    100 g (4 oz) cheese, grated
    milk to glaze

Roll out the pastry dough on a lightly-floured board and line a
20-cm (8-in) flan ring on a baking sheet. Trim the edges and
prick the base with a fork. Re-roll the trimmings and cut them
into 1-cm (½-in) strips and set aside.

Arrange the butter beans in the flan case. Beat together the
eggs, milk and yoghurt, season with salt and pepper and fork
in the chives and cheese. Pour over the beans. Brush the dough
edge with milk. Arrange the dough strips in a lattice pattern
over the top of the filling and brush with milk.

Bake in the oven preheated to 200°C (400°F), Gas 6, for
40–45 minutes, until the custard is set and the top is golden

brown. Serve warm garnished, if you like, with more chopped chives.

Serves 4

CREAM CHEESE AND VEGETABLE FLAN

As light and summery as strawberries and cream, a savoury tart to serve for a sunny-day lunch or buffet.

175 g (6 oz) plain flour
2.5 ml (½ teaspoon) salt
75 g (3 oz) butter
75 g (3 oz) cheese, grated
30 ml (2 tablespoons) water
175 g (6 oz) cream cheese
2 eggs, beaten
300 ml (½ pint) milk
freshly-ground black pepper
225 g (8 oz) broad beans, cooked
100 g (4 oz) peas, cooked
100 g (4 oz) spinach, cooked
2 large tomatoes, sliced

To make the cheese pastry, mix the flour and salt together, cut in the fat and rub it in until the mixture resembles fine breadcrumbs. Mix in the cheese. Add the water and mix to a stiff dough. Cover the paste and chill for at least 30 minutes. Roll out on a lightly-floured board into a circle about 35 cm (14 in) in diameter. Line a greased 30-cm (12-in) flan case. Prick the base with a fork and trim the edges. Line the dough with foil and fill with baking beans. Put the flan case on a baking sheet and bake 'blind' in the oven preheated to 200°C (400°F), Gas 6, for 15 minutes. Remove the foil and beans.

To make the filling, beat the cream cheese until it is smooth, gradually beat in the eggs and milk and season with salt and pepper. Arrange the cooked and drained vegetables neatly in the base of the flan case and pour the cheese filling over. Arrange the tomato slices on top. Return the flan to the oven and bake for about 35 minutes, until the pastry is set and the filling is cooked.

Serves 6–8

VEGETABLE PIE

The kind of dish that's useful for the long and hungry school holidays.

200 g (7 oz) bought puff pastry
2 large carrots, peeled and diced
225 g (8 oz) French beans, trimmed and halved
1 medium-sized onion, peeled and sliced
1 × 600-g (1 lb 4-oz) can baked beans in tomato sauce
10 ml (2 teaspoons) made mustard
15 ml (1 tablespoon) Worcestershire sauce
beaten egg to glaze

Roll out the pastry dough on a lightly-floured board and set aside to rest. Cook the prepared vegetables together in boiling, salted water for about 8–10 minutes, until they are almost tender, and drain them. Mix the baked beans, mustard and sauce together, and gently fold in the vegetables. Turn the filling ingredients into a 1-litre (1½-pint) pie dish.

Dampen the edges of the dish. Cut off a 2.5-cm (1-in) strip all round the dough and press it on to the edges of the dish. Dampen the strip and lift the dough lid in place. Re-roll the trimmings and cut leaves. Dampen the underside and arrange them to decorate the pie. Brush the top with beaten egg to glaze. Bake in the oven preheated to 200°C (400°F), Gas 6, for 25 minutes, until the pastry is golden brown.

Serves 4–6

8   Other Main Dishes

Beans with lamb – a classic of Middle-Eastern dishes; beans with pork, a legacy of traditional dairy and farmhouse fare; beans with beef – shades of cowboys and cattle drovers; beans with rabbit, in a pot over a gypsy camp fire; beans with other vegetables, eggs, pasta, cheese, pancakes. Beans, in fact, with everything.

Bean-feasters will adapt the recipes to their own time scale. Where beans are one of the main ingredients, they are usually listed as pre-soaked, ready to be cooked with the other items. But if it is more convenient, you can easily cook them a day or more in advance and leave them covered in the refrigerator. Or opt for canned ones, and completely eliminate the greatest part of the cooking time. Where fresh beans and peas are recommended, you can naturally choose frozen or canned ones if you wish. The more you become accustomed to adapting the recipes to suit your own life-style, the more versatile your cooking will become – and, as a consequence, the beans themselves.

LEG OF LAMB WITH HARICOT BEANS

A delicious French country dish, beautifully balanced and delicately flavoured.

450 g (1 lb) dried green or white haricot beans, soaked
3 medium-sized onions, peeled
2 cloves
1 bay leaf
a few parsley stalks
1 small leg of lamb, about 1.5 kg (3½ lb)
2 cloves garlic, peeled and thinly sliced
50 g (2 oz) butter
150 ml (¼ pint) dry cider or water
salt and freshly-ground black pepper
15 ml (1 tablespoon) fresh chopped parsley

Drain the beans and cook them in boiling, unsalted water with
1 of the onions stuck with the cloves, the bay leaf and parsley
stalks, until they are just tender – about 1–1½ hours. Drain
them, discarding the onion and herbs, and keep them warm.

Make slits in the lamb with a small, sharp knife and push
slivers of garlic into the meat. Melt the butter in a small
roasting pan and brown the lamb evenly all over. Remove the
lamb and set aside to keep warm. Slice the remaining onions
and add them to the pan. Stir well to coat them in butter and
cook until they are just beginning to brown. Return the lamb
to the pan, pour on the cider or water and season with salt and
pepper. Roast in the oven preheated to 190°C (375°F), Gas 5,
for 1 hour.

Stir the beans into the pan and cook for a further 45 minutes,
or until the lamb is tender. Transfer the lamb to a heated
serving dish and surround it with the beans. Sprinkle the beans
with the parsley before serving.
Serves 6

CASSOULET

A dish that takes quite a bit of time and trouble, but is perfect
for an informal supper party.

    550 g (1¼ lb) dried white haricot beans, soaked
    2 large onions, peeled and chopped
    4 cloves garlic, peeled and crushed
    2 bay leaves
    about 2.5 litres (4 pints) unsalted chicken stock, or water and
        stock cubes
    freshly-ground black pepper
    450 g (1 lb) belly of pork, skinned and cut into thin strips
    450 g (1 lb) lean lamb, cubed
    225 g (8 oz) chorizo sausage, skinned and diced
    1 × 375-g (14-oz) can peeled tomatoes
    5 ml (1 teaspoon) dried oregano
    30 ml (2 tablespoons) tomato purée
    175 g (6 oz) fresh white breadcrumbs

Drain the beans and put them in a large pan with the onions,
garlic, bay leaves and stock – there should be twice the volume

of stock to beans – and bring to the boil. Cover the pan and simmer over a low heat for 1 hour. Drain the partly-cooked beans, reserving and straining the stock.

Put a layer of the beans in the bottom of a very large casserole and season with pepper. Cover with the pork, more beans and pepper, the lamb, more beans and sausage. Stir the oregano into the canned tomatoes and pour the mixture over the sausage. Cover with a final layer of beans. Stir the tomato purée into some of the reserved stock and pour it into the casserole – add more until it just covers the top layer of beans. Sprinkle half the breadcrumbs over the beans.

Put the casserole on a baking tray and cook it, uncovered, in the oven preheated to 150°C (300°F), Gas 2, for 3 hours. Check from time to time and add more reserved stock to keep the level topped up. Push down the breadcrumbs, which will now have formed a crust, with the back of a large spoon, and sprinkle on the remaining breadcrumbs. Return to the oven and cook for a further 45 minutes.
Serves 8

MUSTARD CASSOULET

A simplified dish of sausage, meat and beans that is full of flavour.

   450 g (1 lb) dried white haricot beans, soaked
   2 chicken stock cubes
   1 large onion, peeled and chopped
   100 g (4 oz) salami, skinned and diced
   1 breast of lamb, skinned and cubed
   225 g (8 oz) belly of pork, skinned and cubed
   salt and freshly-ground black pepper
   1 × 375-g (14-oz) can peeled tomatoes
   6 slices of French bread
   45 ml (3 tablespoons) Meaux mustard

Drain the beans and cook them in boiling water with the stock cubes and onion until they are just tender – about 1–1½ hours. Drain them and reserve the liquid.

In an ovenproof casserole, arrange layers of meat and the beans, seasoning each layer with salt and pepper. Pour on the

tomatoes and their juice and a little of the reserved bean stock.
Cover the casserole and cook in the oven preheated to 180°C
(350°F), Gas 4, for 1½ hours. Spread the slices of French bread
with the mustard and arrange them on top of the casserole,
adding a little more liquid if needed. Return uncovered to the
oven and cook at 150°C (300°F), Gas 2, for 30 minutes, until
the bread is brown and crisp.
Serves 6

COUSCOUS

Chick peas are an essential ingredient of this North African
dish. Once you have mastered the method, you can vary the
meat, vegetable and spice combination at will. A pan called a
couscoussier is traditional, but a steamer or a colander fitted
over a saucepan will do perfectly well.

  100 g (4 oz) dried chick peas, soaked
  2 chicken pieces
  675 g (1½ lb) shoulder of lamb
  salt and freshly-ground black pepper
  45 ml (3 tablespoons) olive oil
  2 large onions, peeled and sliced
  2 cloves garlic, peeled and finely chopped
  2 small turnips, peeled and diced
  4 medium-sized carrots, peeled and sliced
  1 green pepper, trimmed and thinly sliced
  1 red pepper, trimmed and thinly sliced
  5 ml (1 teaspoon) paprika
  5 ml (1 teaspoon) ground cumin
  5 ml (1 teaspoon) ground coriander
  2.5 ml (½ teaspoon) cayenne pepper
  2.5 ml (½ teaspoon) ground ginger
  a few threads of saffron, soaked in 15 ml (1 tablespoon) hot
      water for 10 minutes
  1.25 litres (2¼ pints) unsalted chicken stock, or water and
      stock cubes
  4 small courgettes, trimmed and thickly sliced
  30 ml (2 tablespoons) tomato purée
  2 *bouquets garnis*

1 × 450-g (1-lb) packet of couscous grains
50 g (2 oz) butter
325 g (12 oz) broad beans (shelled weight)
30 ml (2 tablespoons) fresh chopped parsley

Cook the chick peas in boiling water for 2 hours. Drain them well and keep warm. Remove the meat from the chicken bones and cut it into chunks. Cut the lamb into cubes. Season well with salt and pepper. Heat 30 ml (2 tablespoons) of oil in a large pan, or the base of a steamer. Fry the meat over a medium heat for 10 minutes, turning frequently to brown evenly. Transfer to a dish to keep warm. In the same pan, fry the onions, garlic, turnips, carrots, green and red pepper for 10 minutes. Stir in the spices and strained saffron water. Cook over low heat for 5 minutes, return the meat to the pan and stir well. Pour on the chicken stock and add the courgettes, chick peas, tomato purée and the *bouquets garnis*. Bring to the boil, stirring. Cover the pan and simmer for 15 minutes.

Tip the couscous grains into a bowl and gradually work in 90 ml (6 tablespoons) water, stirring with a fork to prevent lumps. Line the top of the steamer or the colander with a double layer of muslin, cheesecloth or a tea towel wrung out in boiling water. Turn the couscous into the cloth, fit the top on the pan and steam, uncovered, for 30 minutes. Stir the grains with a fork from time to time.

Turn the couscous into a heatproof mixing bowl that will fit over the pan. Gradually fork in a further 90 ml (6 tablespoons) water, the remaining 15 ml (1 tablespoon) olive oil and 2.5 ml ($\frac{1}{2}$ teaspoon) salt.

Stir the broad beans and parsley into the vegetables in the pan, and add a little more boiling water if necessary. Place the bowl over the pan, cover with a lid or foil and cook for a further 30 minutes. Stir the butter into the couscous grains.

To serve, discard the *bouquets garnis*, transfer the vegetables to a heated serving dish with a draining spoon, and pile the couscous grains round them. Boil the sauce in the uncovered pan for a moment or two to thicken it, if necessary, and serve it separately.

Serves 6

LENTIL HOT-POT

One of those warming, welcoming winter dishes that's a complete meal in a pot.

25 g (1 oz) dripping
450 g (1 lb) middle neck of lamb, trimmed and cubed
1 large onion, peeled and sliced
1 large leek, trimmed, well washed and sliced
2 medium-sized carrots, peeled and sliced
1 small turnip, peeled and diced
1.25 litres (2¼ pints) chicken stock
100 g (4 oz) lentils, washed
1 bay leaf
salt and freshly-ground black pepper

For Scone Topping
225 g (8 oz) flour
10 ml (2 teaspoons) baking powder
2.5 ml (½ teaspoon) celery seeds
2.5 ml (½ teaspoon) celery salt
50 g (2 oz) butter
about 75 ml (5 tablespoons) milk
a little extra milk to glaze
25 g (1 oz) medium oatmeal

Melt the dripping in a flameproof casserole and fry the lamb, turning often until the pieces are evenly browned. Remove the lamb and keep warm. Fry the onion, leek, carrots and turnip over a medium heat for 3–4 minutes, then return the lamb to the pan. Pour on the stock, add the lentils and bay leaf, stir well and bring to the boil. Cover the pan and cook in the oven preheated to 170°C (325°F), Gas 3, for 1¼ hours. Season with salt and pepper, remove the bay leaf, and place the scone round on top. Increase the heat to 200°C (400°F), Gas 6, and cook for 20–25 minutes, until the scone is well risen and golden brown.

To make the scone topping, sift together the flour, baking powder and seasonings into a bowl. Cut in the butter and rub it in until the mixture resembles fine breadcrumbs. Pour on just enough milk to give a soft but not sticky dough. Roll out the dough on a lightly-floured board and shape to fit the top of

the casserole. Mark it into four wedge-shaped portions with a sharp knife. Place it on top of the casserole, brush it with milk and sprinkle it with oatmeal.
Serves 4

OLD-FASHIONED LAMB STEW

There's a special affinity between lamb and butter beans, garnished here with onion dumplings.

25 g (1 oz) dripping
1.25 kg (3 lb) neck of lamb, trimmed and cubed
2 large onions, peeled and sliced
2 large carrots, peeled and sliced
2 small turnips, peeled and diced
10 ml (2 teaspoons) crushed dried rosemary
freshly-ground black pepper
750 ml (1¼ pints) chicken stock, or water and stock cube
225 g (8 oz) dried butter beans, soaked and drained
salt
15 ml (1 tablespoon) fresh chopped parsley
25 g (1 oz) butter
25 g (1 oz) flour

For the Onion Dumplings
50 g (2 oz) butter
1 large onion, peeled and grated
1 egg
100 g (4 oz) fresh white breadcrumbs
50 g (2 oz) self-raising flour
a pinch of dried thyme

Heat the dripping in a large pan and fry the meat over a medium heat, turning it until it is evenly browned. Remove the meat and keep it warm. In the same pan, fry the onions over a medium heat for 5 minutes, add the carrots and turnips and fry for a further 3 minutes. Add the rosemary and pepper, stir in the chicken stock and bring to the boil, skimming off any scum from the surface with a draining spoon. Cover the pan and simmer for 45 minutes. Add the butter beans and continue simmering for 1 hour. Stir in salt, parsley, and the butter and flour worked to a paste. Add the dumplings and cook for a further 20–25 minutes (about 2 hours 10 minutes in all) until the dumplings rise to the top and are well cooked.

To make the dumplings, melt the butter in a small pan and fry the onion over a medium heat until it is transparent. Beat the egg in a mixing bowl and add the butter and onion, breadcrumbs, flour, thyme, and salt and pepper. Beat well, then shape into eight balls. Drop them into the pan, cover, and continue simmering, as described.

Serves 4

PASTA HOT-POT

A complete meal in a pot – perfect to cook in an electric crockpot.

30 ml (2 tablespoons) vegetable oil
2 medium-sized onions, peeled and thinly sliced
1 kg (2¼ lb) middle neck of lamb, trimmed and cubed
1.25 litres (2¼ pints) chicken stock, or water and stock cube
juice and grated rind of 1 orange
30 ml (2 tablespoons) fresh chopped mint leaves
freshly-ground black pepper
2 medium-sized courgettes, trimmed and thickly sliced
175 g (6 oz) split peas, soaked and drained
175 g (6 oz) pasta shells
salt

Heat the oil in a large, heavy-based saucepan and fry the onions over a medium heat until they are golden brown. Add the lamb and fry, turning it frequently until it is evenly browned. Pour on the stock and add the orange juice and rind, mint and pepper. Bring slowly to the boil, skimming off any scum from the surface with a draining spoon. Cover the pan and simmer for 1 hour. Add the courgettes and split peas, cover and simmer for a further 30 minutes. Add the pasta shells, season with salt and more pepper if needed, cover again and continue simmering for about 30 minutes, until the peas and pasta are tender.

Serves 6

RED SEA CASSEROLE

A one-pot dish that is best made a day in advance.

30 ml (2 tablespoons) vegetable oil
2 medium-sized onions, peeled and sliced
4 stalks celery, thinly sliced
2 large carrots, peeled and sliced
1 kg (2¼ lb) middle neck of lamb, trimmed and cubed
25 g (1 oz) flour
freshly-ground black pepper
5 ml (1 teaspoon) dried thyme
15 ml (1 tablespoon) tomato purée
600 ml (1 pint) unsalted chicken stock, or water and stock
    cube
1 large aubergine, trimmed, sliced and dégorged
100 g (4 oz) dried white haricot beans, soaked and drained
salt

Heat the oil in a large flameproof casserole and fry the onions, celery and carrots over a medium heat for 4–5 minutes. Remove the vegetables with a draining spoon and set aside to keep warm. Toss the lamb in flour seasoned with pepper and the dried thyme, and fry in the pan, turning frequently to brown evenly. Return the cooked vegetables to the pan and stir in the tomato purée and chicken stock. Add the aubergine and haricot beans. Bring to the boil, cover the pan and simmer for 2½ hours, or cook in the oven preheated to 170°C (325°F), Gas 3. Taste and adjust seasoning. If possible, make the dish a day in advance, leave it to cool and lift off the layer of fat from the top, then reheat to serve. Otherwise, skim off the surface fat with a draining spoon.

Serves 4

TUNISIAN HOT-POT

Dried fruit and spices make this a truly North African dish. You can use ready-cooked or canned chick peas.

  40 g (1½ oz) butter
  1.25 kg (3 lb) leg of lamb, cubed
  2 large onions, peeled and sliced
  2 cloves garlic, peeled and crushed
  1 red pepper, trimmed and thinly sliced
  5 ml (1 teaspoon) ground cumin
  5 ml (1 teaspoon) ground coriander
  2.5 ml (½ teaspoon) chilli powder
  2.5 ml (½ teaspoon) ground allspice
  salt and freshly-ground black pepper
  450 ml (¾ pint) chicken stock, or water and stock cube
  50 g (2 oz) dried apricots, soaked and drained
  50 g (2 oz) dried prunes, soaked, drained and stoned
  50 g (2 oz) seedless raisins
  50 g (2 oz) sultanas
  225 g (8 oz) dried chick peas, cooked and drained

Melt the butter in a large frying-pan and fry the lamb cubes, a few at a time, until they are evenly browned. Remove them with a draining spoon, transfer them to a flameproof casserole and keep them warm.

In the same pan, fry the onions, garlic and red pepper over a medium heat, until the onions are golden brown. Transfer the vegetables to the casserole and place over a medium heat. Stir in the spices and seasoning and cook for 3–4 minutes. Pour on the chicken stock, stirring, and bring to the boil.

Cover the casserole and continue simmering gently, or cook in the oven preheated to 170°C (325°F), Gas 3, for 45 minutes. Add the dried fruits and the chick peas, stir well, cover and cook for a further 30 minutes.
Serves 6

DRUGSTORE CHICKEN

Colourful, slightly sweet, and full of fruit – a favourite with children. And a good way to use up Sunday's meat.

30 ml (2 tablespoons) vegetable oil
1 large onion, peeled and chopped
5 ml (1 teaspoon) chilli powder
1 × 375-g (14-oz) can peeled tomatoes
1 × 447-g (15¾-oz) can baked beans in tomato sauce
450 g (1 lb) cooked chicken, sliced
salt and freshly-ground black pepper
1 × 447-g (15¾-oz) can sliced peaches
15 ml (1 tablespoon) fresh chopped parsley

Heat the oil in a flameproof casserole and fry the onion over a medium heat for 4–5 minutes. Stir in the chilli powder and cook for a further 2 minutes, then stir in the tomatoes and their juice, the baked beans and the chicken. Season well with salt and pepper, cover the casserole and cook in the oven preheated to 180°C (350°F), Gas 4, for 30 minutes. Stir in the peaches and thin the sauce with a little of the syrup. Taste and adjust the seasoning. Return to the oven to heat the peaches through. Garnish with chopped parsley before serving.
Serves 4

SPICED BEAN CHICKEN

40 g (1½ oz) butter
4 chicken pieces, skinned
2 medium-sized onions, peeled and sliced
1 green pepper, trimmed and sliced
15 ml (1 tablespoon) paprika
300 ml (½ pint) chicken stock, or water and stock cube
30 ml (2 tablespoons) tomato purée
1 × 200-g (7-oz) can peeled tomatoes
5 ml (1 teaspoon) dried oregano
5 ml (1 teaspoon) sugar
salt and freshly-ground black pepper
1 × 220-g (7¾-oz) can baked beans
150 ml (¼ pint) fresh soured cream
5 ml (1 teaspoon) fresh chopped parsley

Melt the butter in a frying-pan and fry the chicken pieces for 5 minutes on each side, until they are golden brown. Transfer them to a casserole. Fry the onions and pepper in the pan over a medium heat for 4–5 minutes, then stir in the paprika and cook for 2 minutes. Stir in the chicken stock and tomato purée, the tomatoes and their juice, oregano and sugar, and season with salt and pepper. Bring to the boil, then pour over the chicken.

Cover the casserole and cook in the oven preheated to 180°C (350°F), Gas 4, for 1 hour. Stir in the beans and return to the oven for a further 15 minutes. Pour the soured cream over the chicken and garnish with the parsley before serving.
Serves 4

RABBIT STEW

The kind of country stew that used to be cooked over an open fire and enjoyed by those who had to live off the fat of the land.

25 g (1 oz) butter
1 large onion, peeled and sliced
1 kg (2¼ lb) rabbit pieces, washed
25 g (1 oz) flour
freshly-ground black pepper
5 ml (1 teaspoon) dried thyme
600 ml (1 pint) chicken stock, or water and stock cube
30 ml (2 tablespoons) Worcestershire sauce
2 large carrots, peeled and sliced
100 g (4 oz) dried white haricot beans, soaked and drained
2 bay leaves
salt

For the Oatmeal Dumplings
75 g (3 oz) self-raising flour
a large pinch of salt
25 g (1 oz) fine oatmeal
40 g (1½ oz) shredded suet
60 ml (4 tablespoons) cold water

Heat the butter in a large pan and fry the onion over a medium heat for 4–5 minutes. Toss the rabbit pieces in the flour seasoned with pepper and thyme and fry them, turning frequently, until they are evenly browned. Add the chicken stock, sauce, carrots, beans and bay leaves and bring to the boil, stirring once or twice. Cover the pan and simmer for $1\frac{1}{4}$ hours. Season with salt. Add the dumplings, cover the pan again and bring the sauce back to the boil. Continue simmering for a further 20–25 minutes, until the dumplings rise to the top and are cooked. Remove the bay leaves.

To make the dumplings, sift together the flour and salt and stir in the oatmeal. Add the suet and mix to a soft dough with the water. Shape into eight balls.

Serves 4

BACON STEWPOT

A casserole with all the warming qualities of a hearty soup.

675 g ($1\frac{1}{2}$ lb) unsmoked bacon collar or slipper joint
40 g ($1\frac{1}{2}$ oz) butter
2 large leeks, trimmed, well washed and sliced
1 small onion, peeled and chopped
25 g (1 oz) flour
450 ml ($\frac{3}{4}$ pint) chicken stock, or water and stock cube
2 medium-sized carrots, peeled and sliced
freshly-ground black pepper
1 × 200-g (7-oz) can butter beans, drained
15 ml (1 tablespoon) fresh chopped parsley

Remove the rind and any excess fat from the bacon and cut the meat into 2-cm ($\frac{3}{4}$-in) dice. Put in a pan with cold water to cover and bring slowly to the boil. Drain, and dry the meat on crumpled kitchen paper.

Melt the butter in a pan and fry the leeks and onion over a low heat for 5–6 minutes. Stir in the flour, then gradually pour on the stock, stirring. Bring to the boil and simmer, still stirring, for 1 minute. Add the carrots, bacon and pepper, cover the pan and cook for $1\frac{1}{4}$ hours. Stir in the beans and parsley and heat through over low heat for about 5 minutes.

Serves 4

SUCCOTASH

When this dish was made in New Zealand, to feed hungry
settlers at the end of a day on the farm, the system was simple –
they counted back four hours from supper time, then started
cooking. The Indians used whole ears of corn, and bear's fat
for flavour.

    225 g (8 oz) dried kidney beans, soaked
    225 g (8 oz) belly of pork, skinned and cubed
    4 chicken pieces, skinned
    2 medium-sized potatoes, peeled and diced
    2 small turnips, peeled and diced
    salt and freshly-ground black pepper
    50 g (2 oz) butter
    225 g (8 oz) frozen sweetcorn, thawed
    150 ml ($\frac{1}{4}$ pint) single cream

Drain the beans and put them in a large pan with the pork and
chicken pieces, and cover with water. Bring to the boil, cover
the pan and simmer for 1 hour, skimming any scum from the
surface with a draining spoon. Add the potatoes and turnips
and simmer for a further 30 minutes. Add the salt, pepper,
butter and sweetcorn, bring back to the boil and simmer for
15 minutes. Remove the pan from the heat, stir in the cream
and taste and adjust seasoning. Reheat without boiling.
Serves 4

BOSTON BAKED BEANS

This is the dish that was cooked over Saturday by American
families, to be eaten on Sunday, a day of rest even from cooking. It was accompanied by steamed wholemeal bread.

    325 g (12 oz) dried red kidney beans, soaked
    15 ml (1 tablespoon) vegetable oil
    1 large onion, peeled and sliced
    1 × 200-g (7-oz) can peeled tomatoes
    15 ml (1 tablespoon) tomato purée
    15 ml (1 tablespoon) molasses or black treacle
    5 ml (1 teaspoon) mustard powder

300 ml ($\frac{1}{2}$ pint) unsalted chicken stock, or water and stock
cube
675 g ($1\frac{1}{2}$ lb) belly of pork, skinned and cubed

Drain the beans and cook them in boiling unsalted water until
they are almost tender – about 1 hour. Drain them well.

Heat the oil in a flameproof casserole and fry the onion over
a medium heat until it is transparent. Add the partly-cooked
beans, tomatoes and their juice, tomato purée, molasses or
treacle, mustard and stock, stir well and bring to the boil.
Arrange the cubes of pork on top, cover the dish and cook in
the oven preheated to 150°C (300°F), Gas 2, for about 5 hours,
stirring occasionally. Taste and season if necessary.
Serves 4

HAND OF PORK WITH PEASE PUDDING

about 1.5 kg ($3\frac{1}{4}$ lb) hand of pork
5 ml (1 teaspoon) dried sage
8 peppercorns
3 large carrots, peeled and quartered
1 large onion, peeled and sliced
3 stalks celery, washed and sliced
1 small turnip, peeled and diced

For the Pease Pudding
450 g (1 lb) split peas, soaked and drained
a mint sprig
25 g (1 oz) butter
1 egg
salt and freshly-ground black pepper

Put the pork in a large pan with the sage and peppercorns tied
in a piece of muslin. Cover with water, bring to the boil, skimming any scum from the surface with a draining spoon. Cover,
simmer for 15 minutes, then add the prepared vegetables.
Simmer for 1 hour before adding the pease pudding.

To make the pudding, tie the peas in a pudding cloth with
the sprig of mint – allow space for the peas to swell. Suspend
the bag in the broth and simmer for 1 hour more. Remove the
pudding, rub the peas through a sieve and beat in the butter,

egg and seasoning. Put the purée in a clean cloth and suspend it in the broth again. Simmer for a further 30 minutes – a total cooking time of 2¾ hours. Remove the pudding to a heated serving dish and cut it in slices.
Serves 4

ITALIAN PORK AND BEANS

If you cannot obtain the peppery boiling sausage, you can make this casserole with 'ordinary' pork sausages, though the flavour will of course be quite different.

    6 rashers streaky bacon, de-rinded and chopped
    10 shallots, peeled, or use small pickling onions
    2 cloves garlic, peeled and crushed
    2 carrots, peeled and sliced
    675 g (1½ lb) dried flageolets, soaked and drained
    450 g (1 lb) Italian spiced boiling sausages
    150 ml (¼ pint) dry white wine
    600 ml (1 pint) unsalted chicken stock, or water and stock
       cube
    2 bay leaves
    a few parsley stalks
    salt and freshly-ground black pepper
    30 ml (2 tablespoons) fresh chopped parsley

In a flameproof casserole, fry the bacon until the fat runs. Add the shallots, garlic and carrots and fry, stirring occasionally, over a low heat for 10 minutes. Add the beans, sausages, wine, stock and the bay leaves and parsley stalks tied together. Bring to the boil, cover the pan and simmer for 2½ hours, or cook in the oven preheated to 170°C (325°F), Gas 3. Remove the herbs, season well with salt and pepper and continue cooking, uncovered, for 15 minutes. Serve garnished with the parsley.
Serves 6

JAMAICAN CHILLI BEANS

A dish that is both sweet and highly spiced, typical of West Indian cooking.

325 g (12 oz) dried white haricot beans, soaked
450 g (1 lb) salt pork, skinned and cubed
30 ml (2 tablespoons) vegetable oil
2 medium-sized onions, peeled and sliced
2 stalks celery, thinly sliced
1 green pepper, trimmed and thinly sliced
1 × 375-g (14-oz) can peeled tomatoes
30 ml (2 tablespoons) molasses or black treacle
60 ml (4 tablespoons) dark rum
5 ml (1 teaspoon) mustard powder
5 ml (1 teaspoon) soft dark brown sugar
2.5 ml (½ teaspoon) chilli powder
salt and freshly-ground black pepper
15 ml (1 tablespoon) fresh chopped parsley

Drain the beans and cook them in boiling, unsalted water until they are almost tender – about 1 hour. Drain them and keep them warm.

Meanwhile, put the pork cubes in a pan, just cover them with water and bring to the boil, skimming any scum from the surface with a draining spoon. Simmer for 5 minutes, then drain, discarding the liquid.

Heat the oil in a flameproof casserole and fry the onions, celery and green pepper over a medium heat for 4–5 minutes. Add the pork cubes and fry, stirring occasionally, for a further 5 minutes. Tip in the tomatoes and their juice, stir well and heat through.

Mix together the molasses or treacle, the rum, mustard, sugar and seasonings and pour over the vegetables. Add the beans, stir well and cover the casserole. Simmer on top of the stove or cook in the oven preheated to 180°C (350°F), Gas 4, for 40–45 minutes, until the sauce is well blended. Serve garnished with the parsley.
Serves 4

JUG-JUG

This is traditionally served in Barbados as an accompaniment to baked ham or roast chicken.

175 g (6 oz) salt beef
175 g (6 oz) lean pork, trimmed of fat
1 × 400-g (15-oz) can gungo peas, drained
2 medium-sized onions, peeled and finely chopped
2 spring onions, trimmed and thinly sliced
2 stalks celery, finely chopped
15 ml (1 tablespoon) chopped celery leaves
15 ml (1 tablespoon) fresh chopped parsley
2.5 ml (½ teaspoon) dried thyme
salt and freshly-ground black pepper
50 g (2 oz) ground millet
50 g (2 oz) butter

Cut the beef and pork into 15 mm (½-in) cubes and put it in a pan with just enough water to cover. Bring the water to the boil, skimming off any scum from the surface with a draining spoon. Cover the pan and simmer for 1 hour. When the meat is cooked, strain off the liquor and reserve it. Mix the gungo peas with the meats and mince them together. Set this purée aside.

Return the reserved stock to the pan with the onions, spring onions, celery, celery leaves, parsley and thyme, and season with salt and pepper. Bring to the boil, cover the pan and simmer for 15 minutes, stirring occasionally. Stir in the meat mixture and ground millet and continue simmering for 20–25 minutes, until the mixture is stiff. Stir in half the butter. Turn the mixture on to a heated serving plate and smooth it into a mound shape. Cut the remaining butter into very small pieces and scatter them on top.
Serves 6

RED PORK AND BEANS

A meal in a dish that needs no more than crisp, crusty bread.

15 ml (1 tablespoon) vegetable oil
2 medium-sized onions, peeled and sliced
1 × 375-g (14-oz) can peeled tomatoes
5 ml (1 teaspoon) dried thyme
salt and freshly-ground black pepper

1 × 225-g (8-oz) can red kidney beans, drained
15 ml (1 tablespoon) red wine vinegar
4 pork chops, trimmed of excess fat
1 large aubergine, trimmed, sliced and dégorged
1 large cooking apple, peeled, cored and sliced

Heat the oil in a frying-pan and fry the onions over a medium heat for 4–5 minutes. Add the tomatoes and their juice, thyme, salt and pepper. Bring to the boil, and simmer for 10 minutes before stirring in the kidney beans and vinegar. Cook for 2–3 minutes more, until the beans have heated through.

Grease a casserole dish and spread half of the tomato mixture over the base. Arrange the chops on top, cover with aubergine and apple slices and season well with salt and pepper. Cover with the rest of the tomato mixture. Cover the casserole and cook in the oven preheated to 180°C (350°F), Gas 4, for 1½–2 hours, until the meat is tender.
Serves 4

BEEF COBBLER

675 g (1½ lb) stewing steak, trimmed and cubed
25 g (1 oz) flour
freshly-ground black pepper
2.5 ml (½ teaspoon) dried mixed herbs
25 g (1 oz) dripping
2 medium-sized onions, peeled and sliced
825 ml (1½ pints) water
10 ml (2 teaspoons) tomato purée
2 medium-sized carrots, peeled and sliced
200 g (7 oz) dried red kidney beans, soaked and drained
salt

For the Topping
225 g (8 oz) self-raising flour
salt and freshly-ground black pepper
a pinch of dried mixed herbs
45 ml (3 tablespoons) cooking oil
150 ml (¼ pint) milk
40 g (1½ oz) porage oats

Toss the meat in a bag with flour seasoned with pepper and herbs. Melt the dripping in a flameproof casserole and fry the onions over a medium heat until they are golden brown. Add the meat and fry, turning frequently until it is evenly browned. Stir in the water and tomato purée, add the carrots and beans, and bring slowly to the boil. Cover the pan and simmer for 2 hours, or cook in the oven preheated to 170°C (325°F), Gas 3. Check and adjust seasoning. Arrange the dough on top of the meat and return the uncovered casserole to the oven. Cook at 190°C (375°F), Gas 5, for 40–50 minutes, until the topping is firm and golden brown.

To make the topping, sieve together the flour, salt and pepper. Add the herbs, oil and milk and mix to a soft dough. Roll tablespoons of the dough in the oats to coat them thoroughly. Arrange the dough on top of the casserole, as described.
Serves 4

CHILLI CON CARNE

Every cook has his own version of this now universal Mexican dish. You can use raw minced beef, substitute canned beans, use chilli powder instead of chillies, what you will.

> 225 g (8 oz) dried red kidney beans, soaked
> 2 medium-sized onions, peeled
> 2 cloves
> 3 cloves garlic, peeled
> 2 dried red chillies
> 30 ml (2 tablespoons) vegetable oil
> 675 g (1½ lb) stewing steak, trimmed and cubed
> 2 red peppers, trimmed and chopped
> 30 ml (2 tablespoons) tomato purée
> salt

Drain the beans and put them in a pan with 1 onion stuck with the cloves, and with 1 peeled and halved clove of garlic. Cook in unsalted water for 1½ hours, then drain the beans, reserving the stock but discarding the onion and garlic. Meanwhile, soak the chillies in hot water for about 1 hour, split them and remove the stalk and seeds. Chop them finely.

Heat the oil in a flameproof casserole. Slice the remaining onion and crush the remaining garlic cloves and fry them over a medium heat for 4–5 minutes. Add the meat, chillies and red pepper and continue to cook, turning frequently, until the meat is evenly browned. Measure 150 ml (¼ pint) of the bean stock, stir the tomato purée into it and pour over the meat. Add the beans, stir well, season with salt and bring to the boil. Cover the pan and simmer for at least 2 hours, or until the meat is cooked and the 'raw' taste of the chillies has gone. Add a little more stock if the dish dries out too quickly.

Serve with boiled rice and a crisp, cooling green salad.
Serves 6

CHILLI BEANS WITH CHEESE

325 g (12 oz) dried red kidney beans, soaked
10 ml (2 teaspoons) red pepper sauce
50 g (2 oz) butter
2 large onions, peeled and chopped
325 g (12 oz) minced beef
25 g (1 oz) flour
1 × 75-g (3-oz) can tomato purée
5 ml (1 teaspoon) chilli powder
300 ml (½ pint) chicken stock, or water and stock cube
175 g (6 oz) full-fat soft cream cheese
15 ml (1 tablespoon) fresh chopped parsley

Drain the beans and cook them in boiling salted water with half of the red pepper sauce until they are almost tender – about 1 hour. Drain them well.

Melt the butter in a flameproof casserole and fry the onions over a medium heat until they are golden brown. Add the minced beef and fry, stirring occasionally, until it is evenly browned. Stir in the flour, tomato purée, the remaining pepper sauce and chilli powder and cook for 2–3 minutes. Pour on the stock, stirring, add the beans and bring to the boil. Cover the casserole and simmer for 30 minutes.

Spoon the cheese on to the casserole in small pieces and serve at once, sprinkled with the parsley.
Serves 4

MEATBALLS WITH BEANS

Not too demanding on time or money, a 'fun' dish for children.

450 g (1 lb) minced beef
50 g (2 oz) fresh white breadcrumbs
2.5 ml ($\frac{1}{2}$ teaspoon) dried basil
salt and freshly-ground black pepper
a pinch of celery seeds
30 ml (2 tablespoons) vegetable oil
1 large onion, peeled and sliced
225 g (8 oz) button mushrooms, wiped and sliced
1 × 447-g (15$\frac{3}{4}$-oz) can baked beans in tomato sauce
a few drops of red pepper sauce

Pound the minced beef in a bowl with a pestle or the back of a wooden spoon until it forms a thick paste. Stir in the breadcrumbs and basil and season with salt, pepper and celery seed. Knead the mixture with your hands to make a firm paste and shape it into balls about 4 cm (1$\frac{1}{2}$ in) in diameter.

Heat the oil in a frying-pan and fry the meatballs, turning them over so that they are evenly browned. Remove them and set aside to keep warm. Fry the onion in the same pan for 4–5 minutes, add the mushrooms and fry for 2 minutes more. Stir in the beans and pepper sauce, return the meatballs to the pan and simmer for 20 minutes. Taste and adjust seasoning.
Serves 4

SPICED CHICK PEAS

The Spanish way of cooking chick peas, in a casserole with fiery peppers and spiced sausage.

325 g (12 oz) dried chick peas, soaked
825 ml (1$\frac{1}{2}$ pints) unsalted chicken stock, or water and stock cube
a pinch of bicarbonate of soda
30 ml (2 tablespoons) olive oil
1 large onion, peeled and thinly sliced
2 cloves garlic, peeled and crushed

2 medium-sized carrots, peeled and thinly sliced
450 g (1 lb) chorizo sausage, skinned and chopped
1 × 175-g (6-oz) can pimentos, drained and chopped (reserve the liquor)
2.5 ml ($\frac{1}{2}$ teaspoon) dried oregano
salt and freshly-ground black pepper

Drain the peas and cook them in the stock with the bicarbonate of soda, adding salt just before the peas are cooked – about 3 hours. Drain them well.

Heat the oil in a pan and fry the onion and garlic over a medium heat for 4–5 minutes. Add the carrots, chick peas, sausage, chopped pimento and the liquid from the can, the oregano and salt and pepper. Stir well, bring to the boil and simmer over low heat for 15–20 minutes for all the flavours to blend.
Serves 6

SAUSAGE AND BEAN HOT-POT

A good dish for a young teenage party.

225 g (8 oz) dried red kidney beans, soaked
225 g (8 oz) dried white haricot beans, soaked
2 large onions, peeled and sliced
1 × 375-g (14-oz) can peeled tomatoes
675 g (1$\frac{1}{2}$ lb) sausages, lightly grilled and halved
300 ml ($\frac{1}{2}$ pint) dry cider
450 ml ($\frac{3}{4}$ pint) chicken stock
5 ml (1 teaspoon) chilli powder
30 ml (2 tablespoons) tomato purée
15 ml (1 tablespoon) cornflour
salt and freshly-ground black pepper

Drain the beans and put them in a large casserole with the onions, tomatoes and their juice and the sausages. Mix together the cider, chicken stock, chilli powder and tomato purée, and blend a little with the cornflour. Stir that into the cider mixture and boil, stirring until thickened. Pour over the casserole and season. Cover the casserole and cook in the oven preheated to 170°C (325°F), Gas 3, for 1$\frac{1}{2}$ hours or until the

beans are tender. Adjust the seasoning. Serve with salad and French bread.
Serves 6

FLAMENCO EGGS

A light lunch or supper dish with a Mediterranean flavour.

30 ml (2 tablespoons) olive oil
1 large onion, peeled and sliced
2 cloves garlic, peeled and crushed
5 ml (1 teaspoon) red pepper sauce
225 g (8 oz) tomatoes, skinned and sliced
75 g (3 oz) fresh green peas, cooked
75 g (3 oz) French beans, cooked and cut into 2.5-cm (1-in) lengths
100 g (4 oz) spiced garlic sausage, skinned and diced
100 g (4 oz) ham, diced
4 eggs
1 red pepper, trimmed and chopped

Heat the oil in a frying-pan and fry the onion and garlic over a medium heat until transparent. Add the pepper sauce and tomatoes and cook for 5 minutes, stirring occasionally. Add the peas, beans, sausage and ham and cook, stirring once or twice, just long enough to heat through.

Turn into a greased ovenproof dish and level the surface. With the back of a spoon, push four indentations and break an egg into each one. Scatter with the red pepper and bake in the oven preheated to 200°C (400°F), Gas 6, for 10–15 minutes, until the eggs are lightly cooked.
Serves 4

REFRIED BEANS WITH TORTILLAS

An every-day Mexican dish, a hash of cooked kidney beans with spicy sausages and cheese. Use it to fill authentic tortillas, or pancakes.

225 g (8 oz) dried red kidney beans, soaked
225 g (8 oz) chorizo sausage, skinned and chopped

1 large onion, peeled and chopped
2 large tomatoes, skinned and chopped
salt and freshly-ground black pepper
2.5 ml (½ teaspoon) chilli powder
50 g (2 oz) cheese, grated

Drain the beans and cook them in boiling, unsalted water until tender – about 1–1½ hours. Drain them well and liquidize them in a blender, or mince them with the fine blade of a mincer.

Meanwhile, fry the chorizo sausage over a low heat for 5 minutes in a non-stick pan without fat. Remove the sausage with a draining spoon and set aside. Heat the fat in the pan and fry the onion over a medium heat for 5–6 minutes. Stir in the tomatoes and seasonings and cook for 10 minutes. Stir in the sausage, bean purée and cheese. Check seasoning, add more if necessary, and gently heat over a very low heat, stirring to prevent the mixture from sticking.

Use the refried beans as a filling for cornmeal or English-style pancakes.
Serves 4–6

PRAWN FU YUNG

Pancakes with the crisp texture of bean sprouts and the delicate flavour of prawns.

225 g (8 oz) fresh bean sprouts (or canned ones, drained and rinsed)
salt
1 small onion, peeled and grated
2 spring onions, trimmed and thinly sliced
100 g (4 oz) prawns, chopped
freshly-ground black pepper
a pinch of cayenne pepper
30 ml (2 tablespoons) cold water
7 eggs, lightly beaten
oil for frying

Blanch fresh bean sprouts for 1 minute in boiling, salted water, then drain. Stir all the ingredients into the eggs.

Heat a heavy-based frying-pan and heat about 5 ml (1 teaspoon) oil. Spoon in just enough egg mixture to cover the pan,

shake well, and cook until it sets. Flip over to cook the other
side. Slide on to a heated serving dish and keep warm while
you cook all the egg mixture.
Serves 4

HAM FRITTERS

    25 g (1 oz) butter
    1 medium-sized onion, peeled and finely chopped
    25 g (1 oz) flour
    150 ml (¼ pint) milk
    175 g (6 oz) cooked ham, finely chopped or minced
    100 g (4 oz) peas, cooked
    2.5 ml (½ teaspoon) mustard powder
    15 ml (1 tablespoon) fresh chopped parsley
    salt and freshly-ground black pepper

    For the Batter
    175 g (6 oz) flour
    1.5 ml (¼ teaspoon) salt
    150 ml (¼ pint) beer
    60 ml (4 tablespoons) water
    oil for frying

Melt the butter in a small pan and fry the onion over a medium
heat for 3–4 minutes. Stir in the flour and cook until it forms a
ball. Gradually pour in the milk, stirring, and bring to the boil.
Simmer until the sauce thickens, then cool. Stir in the ham,
peas, mustard, parsley and seasoning. Remove from the heat,
cover and leave to chill for about 30 minutes. Flour a board
and shape the fritter paste into eight sausage shapes. Roll them
in flour to coat them.

Make the batter just before it is needed. Mix the flour and
salt together. Add half the beer and beat well. Beat in the
remaining beer and water and season with salt. Coat the
fritters in the batter. Pour a little oil into a frying-pan and
shallow fry the fritters, turning them until they are evenly
golden brown.

Serve the fritters with grilled tomatoes and green salad.
Serves 4

STEAMED PORK LOAF

An unusual steamed meat pudding, complete with pasta and vegetables, a perfect example of traditional farmhouse food.

675 g (1½ lb) lean pork, minced
1 × 375-g (14-oz) can peeled tomatoes, drained
30 ml (2 tablespoons) tomato purée
1 clove garlic, peeled and crushed
salt and freshly-ground black pepper
a pinch of grated nutmeg
5 ml (1 teaspoon) dried oregano
175 g (6 oz) short-cut macaroni, cooked and drained
175 g (6 oz) fresh green peas, cooked (or use frozen ones)
1 egg, lightly beaten

Beat the minced pork and tomatoes together, then beat in the tomato purée, garlic, seasonings and oregano. Stir in the macaroni and peas and bind with the beaten egg.

Grease a 1.25-litre (2¼-pint) pudding basin and turn the mixture in. Level the top, cover with greased greaseproof paper or foil leaving room for expansion and then with a greased pudding cloth. Tie securely and place on a trivet in a pan of boiling water. Steam for 2½ hours. Serve with crusty French bread.

Serves 4–6

PASTA PIE

A good party dish that can be made a day in advance.

325 g (12 oz) dried chick peas, soaked
a pinch of bicarbonate of soda
salt
2 medium-sized aubergines
about 45 ml (3 tablespoons) olive oil
1 large onion, peeled and sliced
2 cloves garlic, peeled and crushed
450 g (1 lb) minced beef
30 ml (2 tablespoons) tomato purée
1 × 375-g (14-oz) can peeled tomatoes
freshly-ground black pepper
10 ml (2 teaspoons) dried oregano
175 g (6 oz) short-cut macaroni
300 ml (½ pint) natural yoghurt
2 eggs, lightly beaten
75 g (3 oz) cheese, grated

Drain the dried chick peas and cook them in boiling water with the bicarbonate of soda, adding salt just before the beans are cooked – about 3 hours. Drain them well and set them aside.

Trim the stalks from the aubergines and slice them diagonally. Sprinkle them with salt and leave them in a colander over a plate to drain for 30 minutes. Wash them in cold water and pat them dry.

Heat the oil in a large frying-pan and fry the aubergine slices on both sides, until they start to change colour. Remove them with a draining spoon and drain on kitchen paper towels while you fry the remaining slices. In the same pan, fry the onion and garlic over a medium heat for 3–4 minutes, add the minced beef and fry, stirring occasionally, until it is evenly browned. Add the tomato purée, the tomatoes and their juice, salt, pepper and oregano and stir well. Bring the mixture to bubbling point, cover the pan and simmer for 25 minutes. Stir in the chick peas and heat through.

Meanwhile, cook the macaroni in plenty of boiling, salted water according to the directions on the packet. Drain it in a colander and refresh it under cold, running water. Drain it again.

To make the sauce, beat the yoghurt, eggs and cheese together and season with salt and pepper. Stir in the macaroni until it is thoroughly coated with the sauce.

Grease a large ovenproof dish and stand it on a baking sheet. Arrange half the aubergine slices in the base, turn the meat and chick pea mixture on top and cover with the remaining aubergine slices. Top with the macaroni sauce, level the surface and bake in the oven preheated to 190°C (375°F), Gas 5, for 35–40 minutes, or until the top is crisp and golden brown.
Serves 6–8

SPICED SAUSAGE AND EGG PIE

An economical dish to make when there's an invasion of children to lunch.

450 g (1 lb) shortcrust pastry
30 ml (2 tablespoons) vegetable oil
2 medium-sized onions, peeled and sliced
30 ml (2 tablespoons) tomato purée
15 ml (1 tablespoon) curry powder
15 ml (1 tablespoon) Worcestershire sauce
2 × 375-g (14-oz) cans baked beans
450 g (1 lb) sausages, cooked and chopped
3 hard-boiled eggs
salt and freshly-ground black pepper
1 egg, beaten, to glaze

Roll out the pastry dough on a lightly-floured board. Reserving a quarter for the lid, line a deep pie dish, trimming the edges. Prick the base with a fork. Mix all the remaining ingredients together (except the beaten egg) and turn into the dish. Dampen the edges and press the pastry lid in place. Re-roll the trimmings and cut them into decorative shapes. Arrange them in place, push a small hole in the lid to allow the steam to escape, and brush with beaten egg to glaze. Place on a baking sheet and bake in the oven preheated to 190°C (375°F), Gas 5, for about 40 minutes, until the pastry is golden brown. Serve hot.
Serves 8

MICHIGAN PASTIES

Cheap and very cheerful, for picnics or packed lunches.

225 g (8 oz) shortcrust pastry
15 g ($\frac{1}{2}$ oz) butter
1 small onion, peeled and chopped
225 g (8 oz) minced beef
2.5 ml ($\frac{1}{2}$ teaspoon) dried mixed herbs
5 ml (1 teaspoon) made English mustard
1 × 200-g (7-oz) can baked beans
salt and freshly-ground black pepper
a few drops of Worcestershire sauce

Roll out the pastry dough on a lightly-floured board and leave it to rest while you make the filling.

Melt the butter in a pan and fry the onion over a medium heat for 4–5 minutes. Add the minced beef and cook, stirring occasionally, until it is evenly browned. Stir in the herbs, mustard and baked beans and season with salt, pepper and the sauce. Bring to the boil and simmer for 10 minutes. Remove the pan from the heat and allow the filling to cool.

Cut the dough into four 12-cm (5-in) squares. Divide the filling between them and pile it into the centre of each square. Dampen the dough edges and bring the four corners to the centre, over the filling. Pinch them together to seal. Roll out the trimmings into four tiny balls and press one on each pasty top. Brush all over with beaten egg and put the pasties on a baking sheet. Bake in the oven preheated to 200°C (400°F), Gas 6, for 25–30 minutes, until the pastry is crisp and golden brown. Serve hot or cold.
Serves 4

SOYA COTTAGE PIE

An example of the way in which soya protein granules, a soya bean product, can be used to 'extend' minced beef.

25-g (1-oz) packet soya protein granules
60 ml (4 tablespoons) water
225 g (8 oz) minced beef

50 g (2 oz) butter
2 stalks celery, thinly sliced
1 medium-sized onion, peeled and chopped
1 medium-sized carrot, peeled and thinly sliced
15 g ($\frac{1}{2}$ oz) flour
300 ml ($\frac{1}{2}$ pint) beef stock, or water and stock cube
salt and freshly-ground black pepper
2.5 ml ($\frac{1}{2}$ teaspoon) dried mixed herbs
15 ml (1 tablespoon) fresh chopped parsley
2 large tomatoes, skinned and quartered
25 g (1 oz) cheese, grated
675 g (1$\frac{1}{2}$ lb) potatoes, mashed

Rehydrate the soya protein granules with water as directed on the packet and mix it with the minced beef.

Melt the butter in a pan and fry the celery, onion and carrot over a medium heat for 3–4 minutes, then stir in the meat mixture and fry for 5–6 minutes, until evenly browned. Stir in the flour and cook for 1 minute. Pour on the stock, season with salt and pepper and stir in the herbs and tomatoes. Bring to the boil, cover the pan and simmer for 20 minutes.

Transfer the meat mixture to a deep pie dish. Stir the grated cheese into the mashed potatoes and spread them over the meat. Level the top and criss-cross the surface with a fork. Put the dish on a baking sheet and bake in the oven preheated to 200°C (400°F), Gas 6, for 20 minutes, until the potatoes are lightly browned.

Serves 4

NOTE: You can use this soya bean product, in this proportion, with minced beef in many other dishes, such as hamburgers, *chilli con carne*, spaghetti Bolognese, and so on.

Jack must have been the best-ever public relations man for the bean and pea family, demonstrating in true fairy-tale fashion that all you have to do is drop a seed casually into the ground, turn your back and, hey presto! The next day you can shin up a beanstalk as tall as a block of high-rise flats.

That's a slight exaggeration, of course, but growing beans and peas is truly one of the delights of gardening, and there's nothing quite as satisfying as that first basket of bright green pods you pick one early summer's day. The seeds you eat are the seeds you sow – comfortingly large and easy to handle for first-time gardeners who are all fingers-and-thumbs, and fairly good tempered into the bargain.

If you have a wall in a sheltered spot, a vegetable patch in your garden, or an allotment, you can go in for tall, stately rows of runner beans which will climb eagerly up the wall or a frame of supporting sticks. When you see your plants a mass of scarlet, white, red and white or purple flowers, you will readily understand why runner beans used to be grown for their decorative properties alone. Some varieties reach for the sky a full 360 cm (12 ft) tall, but if your garden would be over-powered by such giant beanstalks, you can pinch out the tops to encourage shorter, bushier plants, or choose a lower-growing variety in the first place.

French beans grow to a middle height, taking their place less obtrusively among other vegetables, or if you opt for one of the really dwarf varieties, you can plant them as an edging to a herb patch or even a flower bed.

Their best friends would probably not describe broad bean plants as decorative. But the greyish-green little beans, fragrant, sweet and tender, are one of summer's loveliest crops and, what's more, they freeze more successfully than practically any other vegetable.

No garden, only a balcony? You can grow runner beans in

deep troughs to climb against the house wall, or in large round tubs, climbing up a wigwam of supporting sticks. French beans grow well in these containers, too, and dwarf varieties can even be grown in a window box, as long as the soil is well fertilized and kept moist.

Not even a balcony? Then open up the pleasures and rewards of indoor gardening, with a nourishing range of bean and pea sprouts grown in boxes, trays or jars in the kitchen, and enlarge your repertoire of cool, slimming salads, warm, hearty soups and casseroles, light, crisp vegetable dishes, and Chinese pancakes, all the better for Oriental-style bean and pea shoots.

GROWING RUNNER BEANS

Runner beans, like all beans and peas, thrive in rich soil which has been dug deeply, and has a good lime content (pH6.5). It pays to think ahead and dig manure into the ground in the autumn. Put off this job until the spring and the soil will be too rich, encouraging growth but not crops. To grow the beans in rows, dig out a trench the depth of a spade (old gardeners used to say 'a spit deep') and about 45 cm (18 in) wide, dig in compost or rotted manure, then fill the trench in again. To grow plants in a round bed, mark out the circular area and dig the manure into the whole patch.

Runner bean seeds are warm-weather merchants and must not be sown until there is no more danger of frost – from early May onwards, according to the season and your locality. Scrape out a drill – a groove – 5 cm (2 in) deep round the perimeter of a circular patch, or in double rows about 30 cm (12 in) apart. Drop the seeds into the drills at 25-cm (10-in) intervals, rake the soil over to cover them, then firm it down with your feet. To plant a second double row of beans, leave a distance between them of the full height the bean plants are to grow.

If you opt for the taller varieties, you can cramp their style by pinching out the main growing shoot when the plants reach about 30 cm (12 in) high. This will encourage the growth of side shoots; to keep the plants low and thickly bushy, pinch out some of these, too. Bean plants do not need much maintenance, but you should hoe between the rows to turf out the weeds, and you must keep the plants well watered. If some of the flowers start dropping off, take it as a timely warning that the plants are not moist enough. Give them a good soaking and sprinkle them with a can of water from above.

Harvest the beans when they are small and young, from about July onwards, to enjoy them at their succulent best.

STAKING YOUR CLAIM

If your garden is rather exposed to the elements, it is probably best to choose lower-growing varieties – tall plants, however well staked, are something of a wind trap. Runner beans need plenty of support – use sticks or long garden canes.

There are two ways to stake a double row of beans. Drive the canes into the ground at intervals between the plants and criss-cross them over near the top, like a guard of honour. Rest supporting canes where the leaning ones cross and bind them firmly with twine. Or drive the canes in along the two rows and form each group of two pairs into a tent shape, tying the four canes firmly together where they cross. Beans planted in a circle can be given a wigwam-shaped frame of sticks. Push them into the ground between the plants, lean them all into the centre of the bed so that they cross near the top, then tie the poles firmly together at the apex.

GROWING FRENCH BEANS

French beans like a light, rich soil – tacky, heavy clay, alas, is not for them. Again, dig the manure in during the autumn or winter, rake the soil over a week or so before sowing, then wait until no more frosts are forecast. Scrape out a drill 5 cm (2 in) deep and plant the seeds 15 cm (6 in) apart. Leave a good 45 cm (18 in) between subsequent rows.

Thin the seedlings to 30 cm (12 in) apart, hoe regularly between them and keep the ground moderately moist. If the soil is in poor condition, it pays to give it an occasional dressing of fertilizer. In late June, spread a thin layer of straw or pieces of black polythene sheeting along the rows, close to the roots. This keeps down weeds and protects low-growing pods. Drive a few twigs along the rows close to the plants to support them as they start to bear their heavy load.

If the plants suffer from an attack of blackfly, spray them with derris in the evening, after the bees have stopped working. Daytime spraying is poor garden husbandry.

To enjoy the fresh, green beans when they are very young and tender, harvest them from July onwards.

HARICOT BEANS

Two varieties of French beans are particularly recommended to grow for drying, Comtesse de Chambord and Brown Dutch. Leave the pods on the plants until the seeds are completely ripe and the pods have faded to a dark creamy-brown. Then lift the whole plants and tie them in bundles close to the roots. Hang the plants in an open but sheltered place – a car-port, open shed or garage, or close against a wall. When the pods are dry and rattle, shell the beans and store them in a cool, dry place.

GROWING BROAD BEANS

Broad beans might be the ugly ducklings of the vegetable garden, but they can be the fairy princesses of a summer meal, sparkling with butter and fragrant with fresh garden herbs.

For very early pickings in the spring, you can sow the seed in November, to stay in the ground over the winter. Choose a rather sheltered spot and hope for the best. Although the plants are hardy, there will be some casualties in a really tough winter. However, you might consider it worth the gamble, not only for the joy of the early vegetables, but to cheat the dreaded blackfly of a feast of young shoots. Early-sown plants make their young shoots before the blackfly get to work, and hopefully the pests will scorn the older, tougher leaves.

After that, you can sow hardy varieties in February and early March, and less hardy ones right through April. To get the best from your ground, you can come on again with a 'catch crop' sown as late as July, perhaps when another crop, such as potatoes, has been lifted. These summer-sown plants will be ready to harvest in September, and out of harm's way before the first frosts.

Having taken the precaution of digging manure into the soil in the autumn, rake it over to make the fine tilth that gardeners crave – until the soil is crumbly, like coarse breadcrumbs. Scrape out little drills 5 cm (2 in) deep, in double rows 25 cm (10 in) apart, and drop in the seeds 20 cm (8 in) apart. Before marking out the next double row, leave a gap of about 90 cm (36 in). Rake over the soil and firm it down with your feet. The plants have a lot of work to do in a short time, so keep them well watered and free of weeds.

Tall-growing varieties of broad beans need support. Drive canes in at intervals along both sides of the rows and tie horizontal lines of twine to enclose the stems.

Now for the scourge of all broad beans, blackfly. Later-sown seeds produce the young shoots just when the blackfly are on the look-out for a juicy meal. In an effort to discourage them, pinch out the young shoots when the plants are about 90 cm (36 in) tall; but they are persistent little beasts and this precaution might not be enough. If you are not entirely anti-sprays, you can spray the plants with derris (available from any garden shop) at weekly intervals.

If you want to serve the beans whole, the tiny pods perhaps in a light, creamy parsley sauce, pick them when they are no more than 10 cm (4 in) long. In any case, pick them when the seeds are small and tender. This isn't the extravagance it sounds, because the more pods you pick the more the plants will produce to replace them. Wash sprayed pods thoroughly.

GROWING SOYA BEANS

Soya beans are not a natural in this cold Northern climate of ours, but some hardy varieties, Fiskeby V, for example, will produce reasonable crops in a good summer.

Let the soil warm up a bit before you sow, from the beginning of May. Sow the seeds 4 cm (1½ in) deep and 8 cm (3 in) apart, with 30 cm (12 in) between subsequent rows. The plants grow to about 30 cm (12 in) in height, so you can use them to edge flower beds or borders.

Pick the pods young if you want to eat them whole, or leave them to develop, three or four plump little seeds to a pod.

To get a quick and foolproof, not to mention weather-proof, crop from soya beans, you can grow fresh young bean sprouts indoors. See the notes at the end of the chapter.

GROWING PEAS

Peas like rich, loamy soil with a good lime content, and appreciate the forethought of manure well dug into it.

To pitch for a crop from the end of May, you can sow seed in October or November, protecting the rows under cloches. A really vicious winter might put an end to them, but many gardeners think it worth a try. If you do not overwinter the seed, you can start sowing from the beginning of March in Southern counties, a month later in the North. Make double rows 5 cm (2 in) deep and 10 cm (4 in) apart, and drop the seeds in at 5-cm (2-in) intervals. Rake the soil back over the drills and firm it down with your feet. Space out subsequent rows according to the height of the plants – those that grow 54 cm (2½ ft) high are planted that distance apart. Mice love pea seed, so dip the seeds in paraffin just before you plant them. It will not harm the seed, but the mice will get the message that there is not exactly a pea feast in store for them.

From the very beginning, the little plants will need protection, in the form of a piece of wire netting, from pigeons and sparrows. Then, as soon as they are about 15 cm (6 in) high, stick twigs or canes to support the vines. Tall-growing strains will need strong canes or twigs, criss-crossed twine or wire, or wire netting. Hoe well between the plants to keep them weed-free, and in dry weather give them a mulch – another word dear to the heart of dedicated gardeners – of about 2.5 cm (1 in) of grass mowings or peat between the rows.

To ward off insects, you can spray the plants with an insecticide at the flowering stage. If you do not take this precaution, once the moths have laid their eggs, they will hatch in the shelter of the developing pods.

Harvest the peas as soon as the seeds fatten the pods. The more you pick, the more there will be.

Mange-tout peas (or sugar peas) benefit from an occasional feed of liquid manure. The pods should be harvested while they are still completely flat, and before the seeds start to develop.

Asparagus peas need a good, sunny position and a good, sunny summer if they are to produce a bumper crop. In a

really bad season, you might have to be content with a flourish
of the pretty deep red flowers.

Pick the pods when they are really small, otherwise you will
wonder what all the fuss is about. Once they develop fully they
become tough, stringy and quite unfriendly. They should be
no more than about 2.5 cm (1 in) long.

GROWING BEAN SPROUTS

Regardless of sun, soil or garden – indeed, without the help of
any of them – you can grow fresh bean sprouts in your kitchen
in a matter of days. You can buy the seed from seed merchants,
or use the dried beans and peas you buy from health food
shops. The very ones you have stored in your kitchen cupboard are bean sprouts in waiting. All dried beans and peas
give a very good return. Mung beans and chick peas give a
yield of about ten times their original weight; soya beans, eight
times; aduki beans, four or five times, and lentils, six times
their packet weight.

Take mung beans, the Chinese bean sprouts. Rinse the little
green beans in water, then leave them to soak for a couple of
days. When the skins begin to burst, spread them out on a
piece of damp towelling, old blanket or cotton wool and put
them in a warm cupboard or drawer – it must be dark – at a
temperature of about 21°C (70°F). They must be kept evenly
and moderately damp, so get into the habit of sprinkling them
with a little water two or three times a day. Not too much,
though, or they will go mouldy. In about five days you should
be rewarded with chubby little shoots. Cut them when they are
about 5 cm (2 in) long.

Another way to grow sprouts is in plain glass jam jars, a
method with great appeal to children. Put 45 ml (3 tablespoons)
of any pre-soaked bean or pea seeds into a 450-g (1-lb) jar and
cover it with a piece of muslin, kitchen J-cloth or nylon. Fill the
jar with tepid water, shake it well and drain off the water. Place
the jar on its side in a drawer (remember it must be in the dark)
but don't let it be out of sight, out of mind. Fill the jar with
tepid water each night and morning, shake it well, and drain off
the water again. Repeat until the shoots burst forth and curl up
around the inside of the jar; then they are ready to eat. Tip

them on to a dish, and marvel at the quickness and simplicity of it all.

Try growing soya beans, chick peas and other pulses in the same way, and go from strength to strength with sprouting seeds of all kinds. Spicy fenugreek makes a fabulous and memorable salad with a faintly curry flavour; alfalfa sprouts, delicious in salads and sandwiches, are rich in vitamins A, B complex, C, D, E, G, and K, contain calcium, iron, sodium and sulphur and are claimed to have a unique cholesterol lowering agent into the bargain. And you can buy an interesting mixture called salad sprouts, a blend of several beans and seeds.

Glossary   The A, B and C of Beans and Peas

A for Aduki; B for Black-eyed Beans; C for Chick Peas. And so it goes on. A whole exciting, colourful and delicious alphabet of foods from all over the world.

Just as each country has its own national dish using fresh seeds or pulses, so they have their own names – the familiar French bean has at least a dozen. And as more and more dried beans and peas are imported and make their appearance in our health food shops or on supermarket shelves, it's a help to have a guide to which are which. Here's an at-a-glance dictionary of both fresh and dried beans and peas in all their variety.

ADUKI BEANS

Tiny round dried brick-red beans, sold in many health food shops. Vegetarians use them to make burgers, flavoured with vegetables and herbs. Their slightly sweet flavour blends well with rich poultry and meat, especially duck, goose and pork.

ASPARAGUS PEAS

Like mange-tout peas, asparagus peas are eaten complete, pod and seeds together, but must be picked when they are very young. The slightly frilled pods have a subtle asparagus flavour. They are also called winged peas.

BEAN SPROUTS

The short, fat crispy white little bean sprouts, so familiar a part of Chinese cooking and so delicious in salads, are grown from mung or soya beans. They can be eaten raw or very lightly cooked, and are available in shops fresh or canned. They are quick and easy to grow indoors.

BLACK BEANS

These small, oval beans have shiny, coal-black skins, but are white inside. They feature prominently in African and South American cooking, so they are usually associated with spicy sauces. They are good in vegetable casseroles and with boiled ham. In America, they are also called turtle beans, and in Cuba, *frijoles negros*.

BLACK-EYED BEANS

Small, white kidney beans with a black spot, these are the traditional ingredient of Hoppin' John, a dish from the American South, in which the beans are mixed with tomatoes, rice and herbs. They are also good with pork and spiced sausages. In their native states they are – confusingly – called black-eyed peas and cow beans.

BORLOTTI BEANS

Brown, speckled beans which cook to a floury consistency, and are good for soups. They are a favourite in Italy where, with onions, ham and cinnamon they make Venetian bean soup. And in Piedmont, they have their own version of baked beans, in which borlotti beans are slow-cooked with bacon and cinnamon overnight on Saturday, to be ready after church on Sunday.

BROAD BEANS

One of the first of summer's vegetables, broad beans are in season in Britain in June, July and August, and are usually eaten fresh. Very young ones may be cooked whole in the pod, but they are usually shelled. The seeds freeze extremely well, and they can be bought frozen or canned. They are not often sold dried in Britain – the way they are usually to be found in Greece and other Southern European countries.

Broad beans are known as fava beans in the United States, from their Latin name, *Vicia faba*. They are also called Windsor beans.

BUTTER BEANS

One of the most familiar of pulses in Britain, these large creamy-white kidney-shaped beans are popular in winter casseroles, soups and stews, particularly those with pork and

bacon. They can also be bought canned. Also called calico
beans in the United States.

CHICK PEAS

These round corn-coloured dried seeds (sometimes called
peas, sometimes beans) are popular from the Arab countries,
across the Mediterranean to Spain and Portugal. Chick pea
purée moistened with olive oil is the Greek and Turkish pâté
or dip called *hummus*; they are served in soups, salads, casseroles, baked in tomato sauce, as a garnish to the North African
cereal dish, *couscous*, in rissoles – in an endless variety of ways.
They are even roasted and finely ground, to be used as a non-
caffeinated coffee-type drink. They are also called ceci peas or
garbanzos.

DHAL

The Indian name for the peas, beans and lentils of the
Leguminosae family. Popularly, usually refers to lentils and
split peas.

FAVEROLLES

A French name for *haricot verts*, French beans. Also called
faverottes, and farioles – all derivations from the Latin.

FIELD BEANS

The 'field' refers to the agricultural cultivation of a small type
of broad bean.

FLAGEOLETS

The French name for one variety of kidney, or haricot bean,
with pale green seeds and long, slender pods, said to resemble
a flute. Available in Britain mainly dried or canned, flageolets
are regarded as the most superior of all pulses.

FRENCH BEANS

French beans have at least as many names as there are seeds in
the pod. They are the ancient bean of the New World, rich in
vitamins and mineral salt, from the plant, *Phaseolus vulgaris*.
When the beans are eaten whole, they are called French or

dwarf beans (referring to their low-growing habit) in Britain, sometimes also green or stringless beans. In America, they are snap or string beans and in France, *haricots verts*. They are best picked small and young, and may be harvested in Britain from July to October.

The seeds dry very well and it was in this form that they were the staple diet of the Americas. The best-known variety are small and white, and are sold in Britain as haricot beans. In America, they are called white beans and varieties include marrow beans, navy beans (small ones, served with monotonous regularity in the U.S. Navy), and pea beans, favoured for the traditional New England dish, Boston baked beans. In France, the dried beans are called *haricots jaunes*.

GUNGO PEAS (OR GUNGO BEANS)
These small, dull-brown dried seeds are used in West African and West Indian dishes, and crop up in 'soul food'. Also called pigeon peas.

HARICOT BEANS
The name given to the dried seeds of French beans.

HORSE BEAN
A coarse type of broad bean cultivated only as animal feed.

KIDNEY BEANS
A general term for the dried seeds of the bean which originated in the New World (see French beans).

LENTILS
Red, yellow, brown, grey or green, lentils are excellent in soups or served as a vegetable purée. Red lentils, the familiar coral-coloured ones, are known as Egyptian lentils; the greeny-brown ones – because of their usage, not cultivation – as German, and grey ones as French. In India, purées made from a variety of lentils (dhal) and flavoured with spices and herbs are particularly popular in the vegetarian south. In Hungary, *Lencsefőzelek* is lentils pepped up with paprika, horseradish and soured cream.

Lentils are the seeds of a leguminous plant, *Lens esulenta*, which originated in Asia and has been cultivated there since pre-historic times. Now this valuable source of protein is also grown in Southern Europe, the Middle East and the United States.

LIMA BEANS

A small, green bean grown in America, very similar to butter beans. It is paired with sweetcorn in the traditional American dish succotash.

LOCUST BEAN

The fruit of a Mediterranean leguminous plant, the locust bean is eaten by man only as a last resort. Normally it is an animal feed. It is the pod said to have been eaten by St. John in the Wilderness.

MADAGASCAR BEANS

See butter beans. This term refers to their country of origin.

MANGE-TOUT PEAS

A particularly sweet variety of pea (*Pisum sativum, saccharatum*) which is eaten fresh, before the seeds fully develop and while the pods are still flat. The literal translation of the French, 'eat all' indicates that the whole pods are eaten. Because of their sweetness, they are sometimes called sugar peas. Also called snow peas in the United States.

MARROW BEANS

An American name for haricot beans, dried French beans.

MUNG BEANS

Dried mung beans are small, round and a most attractive bright green which fades a little with cooking. They are delicious in soups, make a good purée and are used to grow bean sprouts. Native to both India and China, from the plant *Phaseolus munga*.

PEAS

As fewer people want to spend time shelling peas, more garden peas (*Pisum sativum*) are becoming field peas, grown commercially for freezing and canning – they were the first vegetables to be processed by these means. They can also be bought dried, in the form which made them a staple part of the diet of ancient civilizations. Peas are easy to grow at home.

PETIT POIS
A small, sweet variety of garden peas, much favoured in France and considered the most succulent of all fresh shelled peas. They can also be bought canned.

PINK BEANS
Brownish-red dried beans, sometimes called red Mexican beans, used in the cooking of the South-western States of America.

PINTO BEANS
Pale pink speckled with dark brown, these dried beans are used in the highly spiced dishes of the American South-west.

RED KIDNEY BEANS
One of the beans that originated in the New World, probably now best known as the 'chilli con carne' bean. The reddish-purple beans can be bought dried or canned, and used not only in that hot, spicy Latin-American way but also in soups, casseroles and salads.

RUNNER BEANS
Another gift to Europe from the New World, runner beans (*Phaseolus coccineus*) crossed the Atlantic about one hundred years after French beans. They are eaten fresh, pods and seeds together, and can be harvested in Britain from July to October. Because of the bright red flowers – which gave rise to the nickname 'scarlet runners' – runner beans used to be grown as a decorative garden plant. Other varieties have purple, white, and scarlet and white flowers, and one – 'Blue Coco' – has violet pods.

SNAP BEANS
A term used to describe French beans, which should be cooked so fresh that they snap when broken in half.

SOYA BEANS

The Soya bean (*Glycine hispida*) is the most important single bean, since it provides first-class protein. They are available dried in Britain, usually a dark beige colour, although they can come in colours ranging from yellow to black. Without a very distinctive flavour of their own, they are used as protein additives in soups, stews and casseroles, cold in salads, and ground in 'burgers and rissoles. They are particularly good with tomato and onion, which add colour and flavour. Bean sprouts can be grown from the seed and both soya sauce and *miso* paste are derived from soya beans.

SPLIT PEAS

A variety of pea is grown specially for drying; in the course of this process the outer cover comes off and the seeds split. Split peas are used to make pease pudding, pea purée and are added to soups.

STRINGLESS BEANS

See French beans. This term distinguishes them from runner beans which, if they are not picked very young, can be tough and stringy.

WHITE BEANS

An American name for haricot beans, dried French beans.

Index

Cooking for good health books now available in Panther Books

Ursula Gruniger
Cooking with Fruit   50p ☐

Sheila Howarth
Grow, Freeze and Cook   £1.50 ☐

Kenneth Lo
Cooking and Eating the Chinese Way   £1.50 ☐
The Wok Cookbook   £1.50 ☐

L D Michaels
The Complete Book of Pressure Cooking   £1.25 ☐

Franny Singer
The Slow Crock Cookbook   £1.50 ☐

Janet Walker
Vegetarian Cookery   £1.50 ☐

Beryl Wood
Let's Preserve It   £1.50 ☐

Gretel Beer and Paula Davies
The Diabetic Gourmet   75p ☐

David Scott
The Japanese Cookbook   £1.50 ☐

Marika Hanbury Tenison
Cooking with Vegetables   £1.95 ☐

Pamela Westland
Bean Feast   £1.50 ☐
High-Fibre Vegetarian Cookery   £1.95 ☐

To order direct from the publisher just tick the titles you want and fill in the order form.

All these books are available at your local bookshop or newsagent, or can be ordered direct from the publisher.

To order direct from the publisher just tick the titles you want and fill in the form below.

Name _____

Address _____

_____

Send to:
Panther Cash Sales
PO Box 11, Falmouth, Cornwall TR10 9EN.

Please enclose remittance to the value of the cover price plus:

UK 45p for the first book, 20p for the second book plus 14p per copy for each additional book ordered to a maximum charge of £1.63.

BFPO and Eire 45p for the first book, 20p for the second book plus 14p per copy for the next 7 books, thereafter 8p per book.

Overseas 75p for the first book and 21p for each additional book.

Panther Books reserve the right to show new retail prices on covers, which may differ from those previously advertised in the text or elsewhere.